SOCIAL SECURITY

The Simplified Beginner's Guide to Social Security

Updated for 2016

ClydeBank
FINANCE

Edition # 1 – Updated : January 31, 2017

Cover Illustration and Design: Katie Poorman, Copyright © 2017 by ClydeBank Media LLC
Interior Design: Katie Poorman, Copyright © 2017 by ClydeBank Media LLC

ClydeBank Media LLC
P.O Box 6561
Albany, NY 12206
Printed in the United States of America

Copyright © 2016
ClydeBank Media LLC
www.clydebankmedia.com
All Rights Reserved

ISBN-13 : 978-0-9963667-2-4

contents

BEFORE YOU START READING, DOWNLOAD YOUR FREE DIGITAL ASSETS!

Be sure to visit the URL below on your computer
or mobile device to access the free digital asset files
that are included with your purchase of this book.

These digital assets will compliment the material
in the book and are referenced throughout the text.

DOWNLOAD YOURS HERE:

www.clydebankmedia.com/socialsecurity-assets

introduction

For many Americans, income from Social Security will provide the majority of their retirement income. Even those who've cultivated other sources of retirement income over the years will still rely largely on Social Security as a significant pillar of their greater financial retirement strategies.

Social Security is the largest source of tax revenue second only to the Federal income tax, and the payout of Social Security benefits is hands down the largest expenditure of the federal government. Whether you've been self-employed, someone's employee, or had your own employees, you've paid into the Social Security system. This means that nearly all Americans are eligible to receive Social Security benefits when they retire. In fact, 97% of Americans are covered by Social Security.

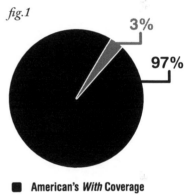

fig.1

3%

97%

■ American's *With* Coverage
■ American's *Without* Coverage

The 3% that never receive benefits can be broken into four categories: infrequent workers, late-arriving immigrants (measured distinctly from infrequent workers), non-covered workers, or workers who die before receiving benefits. The first two categories—infrequent workers and late-arriving immigrants—compose over 80% of 'never beneficiaries' and are also among the poorest levels of society. Non-covered workers are many government employees and employees of the non-profit sector. This category is discussed later in this book.

If you're an employee, then your share consists of a 6.2% withholding of your earnings from your regular paycheck, and your employer pays an additional 6.2% on your behalf for a combined Social Security contribution of 12.4%. If you're self-employed, then you're responsible for paying both your personal share and the employer's share, making your total contribution the entire 12.4% of your earnings. On the bright side for the self-employed, the 6.2% employer's share can be written off as a tax-deductible business expense.

Social Security payments are collected through a payroll tax called 'FICA" which stands for the *Federal Insurance Contributions* Act. For the self-employed, the tax is known as 'SECA" or the *Self-Employed Contributions Act*. Earnings are taxed up to a specific earnings cap, which changes every year. As of 2015, the earnings cap is $118,500, meaning that any income earned as an employee in excess of $118,500 is not subject to Social Security withholding through the FICA or SECA taxes.

This cap changes every year to keep pace with the changing value of our currency. As time goes on, goods and services cost more through *inflation*, and this process happens whether or not the government or anyone else is paying attention. Unless there are provisions in place to make adjustments, the American workforce will slowly lose earning power over time. The *Cost of Living Adjustment*, or COLA, is a provision of the Social Security program that helps protect working Americans from this problem. While it may seem as though an ever-rising cap on FICA taxable income means that the Social Security funds are cheating themselves, many employers offer a baseline annual salary increase (normally between 1-4%) that also increases an employee's wages to match the pace of inflation. The end result: a system that more or less keeps pace with itself and in theory doesn't damage the earning (or spending) power of workers.

Social Security operates like a *pay-as-you-go* system. Money that is withheld from the incomes of working Americans is immediately paid out to retirees and other beneficiaries. This method is distinct from pensions, which are pre-funded, meaning that the money paid into them is set aside to be disbursed to today's workers upon their retirement. Pensions operate this way in order to provide workers with a guaranteed payout in the event the company issuing the pension goes out of business or otherwise becomes unable to pay.

The issuing authority for Social Security benefits is the US *Social Security Administration* (SSA). The SSA handles the receipt and payment of hundreds of billions of tax dollars each year. When Social Security funds are collected—from payroll taxes or elsewhere—the money is credited to Social Security trust funds. These funds are required by law to be set aside for the fulfillment of pledged Social Security benefits. A Board of Trustees oversees these trust funds. Members of the Board of Trustees include the Secretary of the Treasury—who acts as the managing trustee—the Secretary of Labor, the Secretary of Health and Human Services, and the Commissioner of Social Security, as well as two public trustees, one republican and one democratic, who are both appointed by the President and confirmed by the Senate.

If Social Security revenues exceed the amount of benefits paid— for example in 2012, the program took in $840 billion and spent only $786 billion—the law requires the surplus to be invested in special-issue treasury bonds, which pay a modest amount of interest. Since purchasing treasury bonds essentially equates to making a loan to the federal government, excess Social Security revenues can thus be used to financially bolster other federal programs. These 'special issue' treasury bonds, however, are benignly distinct from the treasury bonds available on the open market. Open market treasury bonds, if sold prior to their maturity, may be subject to losses depending on market conditions. The 'special issue' bonds available to the Social Security trust fund are always redeemable at any time for face value. If held to maturity, they are subject to repayment in *principle* and interest. As of 2013, the Social Security trust fund's portfolio maintained an interest value of 3.79%.

A Brief History of Social Security

President Franklin D. Roosevelt signed the Social Security Act into law on August 14, 1935 as part of his 'New Deal' package. Originally intended to rescue the country from the throes of the Great Depression, the Social Security Act (SSA) guaranteed income to the unemployed and retirees. Roosevelt called the program 'patriotic' and expressed concern for young people in the midst of the depression who pondered the fates that awaited them in old age.

For four decades, the only major changes to Social Security came in the form of expansions. Many expanded applications were added even before the program's original mandates were first put into action. In 1939, just as the old-age insurance component of Social Security was getting off the ground, certain family-centric amendments to the program were made. These included an extension of monthly benefits to retired workers' dependents and survivors which were essential to households that lost their primary source of income. The term Old-Age and Survivors Insurance (OASI) was coined and eventually became the formal title of one of the two main Social Security trusts, the OASI Trust Fund, the other being the *Disability Insurance* (DI) Trust Fund[1].

Congress established the Disability Insurance (DI) program in 1956 after decades of debate and discussion on the issue. Some of the sources of contention included how best to define 'disability' and how a person's claimed disability could be verified in a cost effective way on a national scale. A definition was eventually established that was distinct from the existing worker's compensation laws and veteran's pension laws. Disability, according to the 1956 expansion of Social Security, was defined as 'inability to engage in any substantial gainful activity by reason of any medically determinable physical or mental impairment

---

[1] It is important to note that each trust fund is responsible primarily for providing benefits to its respective namesake demographic.

which can be expected to result in death or to be of long-continue and indefinite duration[2].' This definition sought to limit fraudulent applicants who weren't prepared to demonstrate, at any given time, a chronic debilitating condition for the rest of their lives.

The 1960s saw the all-important addition of Medicare to Social Security when President Lyndon Johnson signed it into law. Prior to the inception of Medicare, 35% of senior citizens (citizens age 65 and older) did not have health insurance. On the private market, the cost of healthcare for a senior citizen was about three times the cost of insurance for younger people. Medicare gave all citizens aged 65 or older healthcare, regardless of their incomes or medical histories.

> As an interesting aside, the federal government used Medicare to spur along the ongoing racial desegregation efforts of the day. Hospitals and physician practices could only be paid Medicare benefits if they desegregated their facilities.

The 1970s saw the first real concerns regarding Social Security's ongoing financial feasibility. A new benefits formula produced a large increase in the amount of benefits being paid. The annual program costs, when charted in relation to *gross domestic product*, showed a three to five percent increase over five years. In 1977 amendments to the Act were made to correct the erroneous benefits formula and to bolster the program's general financial architecture.

The debate begun in the 1970s continued into the 80s, culminating in the formation of a commission chaired by renowned economist Alan Greenspan. The Greenspan Commission, as it would come to be known, produced a report recommending changes to the benefits issued and taxes collected on the program's behalf. A 1983 amendment to the Act put the commission's recommendations into law. These reforms caused the program to generate large surpluses and grow trust funds. Nevertheless, the pending retirement of the baby boomers along with

---

[2] The Social Security Definition of Disability, The Social Security Advisory Board, October 2003. p. 3.

various other factors may, by some projections, see the full depletion of the trust funds by the year 2042.

Challenges Ahead

The baby boomers were so named for the Post-World War II 'baby boom' between 1946 and 1964, which created a staggering spike in the country's birth rate. We are currently experiencing the front-end of the baby boomer retirement period, with the first boomers reaching retirement age (62) in 2008. As we wade further into the depths of baby boomer retirement, the amount of Social Security benefits that need to be paid will rise faster than the available tax income. There will be more Americans of retirement age than there will be working Americans of all ages. The fact that post-retirement life expectancy for boomers is longer than that of any previous generation exacerbates the issue.

The "population pyramid" demonstrates how population distribution is currently impacting Social Security. Essentially, this visual chart shows the concentrations of different age groups in a given population. In the United States, we have a relatively longer life expectancy than some other countries (Sierra Leone for example has an average life expectancy of 57.79[3] compared to the 78.74 that the US currently enjoys[4]) and therefore the pyramid may be

No matter the height of the pyramid, the distribution is universally a base of young people that tapers into a peak of dwindling numbers of older citizens. This is the lynchpin of the Social Security system: a larger number of working adults than elderly dependents who rely on the continual funding of the current workforce (pay-as-you-go) (*fig. 2*).

No matter the height of the pyramid however the distribution is naturally roughly the same; a base of young people that tapers into a peak of dwindling numbers of older citizens. This is the lynchpin of

---

[3] Source: Sierra Leone, Selected Statistics 2015 from geoba.se *http://www.geoba.se/country.php?cc=SL*

[4] Source: Data compiled on the behalf of Google with primary sources including the World Bank

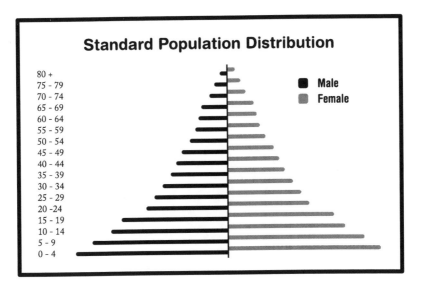

fig. 2 : A standard population distribution. Note the pyramid shape; a wide base of youth that tapers toward old age.

the Social Security system; that there is a larger number of working adults than elderly dependents who rely on the continual funding of the current workforce (pay-as-you-go).

A particularly large generation, such as the baby boomers, can distort the population pyramid. The increase in births so many years ago is now creating a surplus of senior citizens. This changes the population pyramid to resemble a rough column with a wide base with many more dependents than the workforce can support (*fig. 3*).

According to the 2013 Trustees report, Social Security's long run deficit amounts to 2.72% of the taxable payroll. This means that the program will need to either increase revenue or cut expenditures in order to remain financially feasible. On the revenue side, an increase in the taxable earnings cap—currently at $118,500—would result in more revenue collected for the system.

Other ideas include raising the tax rates on employees and employers by a total of about 3%. This increase would be split between

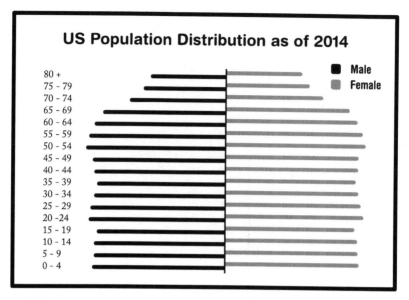

 fig. 3 : The current population distribution of the US. Note the heavily distorted pyramid shape where there are significantly higher levels of middle aged and older citizens.

employees and employers with each party paying and additional one and a half percent more off the payroll. One of the more highly politicized solutions is the idea of investing Social Security funds in the stock market as equities. While many conservatives see this latter option as sensible, progressives tend to view it as reckless; their concern being that no market is stable enough to entrust the futures of millions of Americans.

Another solution still that would improve the disparity between beneficiary recipients and the working population is to extend Social Security coverage to the 25% of state and local government employees who currently do not participate in the system. The idea here is that the addition of more payroll dollars covered by Social Security would mean a larger pool of money to which FICA tax can be applied. The theory is that the gains on the payroll tax end would help close the financial gap now and extend the overall life of the Social Security program.

The amount of benefits paid out can be reduced by raising the eligibility age for full and early retirement benefits, which can be adjusted perpetually in response to the ever increasing life expectancy of Americans. Other approaches include lowering the cost-of-living adjustment and changing benefits so that they are specifically commensurate with price increases rather than wage increases as wage increases have been sluggish and even stagnant for many periods.

While it's beneficial to be aware of what changes may be in store for the Social Security system as a whole, this book is primarily devoted to helping individuals understand how Social Security fits into their overall financial and retirement plans. Many factors will affect your strategy, such as when you plan to retire, whether you're single or married, and the amount of earnings you have invested in the system. This book will walk you through an extensive assessment of how to understand and best manage your Social Security benefits.

| 1 |

The What, When & Who

Unless you're comfortable living off of fifteen thousand dollars a year, you will need to have more components to your retirement plan than just the benefits offered by Social Security. The average benefit for a retired worker in 2013 was $1,263 a month or $15,168 per year. For disabled workers, that average goes down to $1,130 a month or $13,560 per year. Widows or widowers who are 60 years old or older received on average $1,217 a month or $14,604 annually. Social Security, at best, is meant to provide retirees with a retirement foundation that can be enhanced with other sources of income such as savings, pensions and post-retirement earnings.

Keep in mind that Social Security benefits are adjusted each year to keep pace with the ever-increasing cost of living. For example in December 2012, Social Security benefits were adjusted upwards by 1.7% as part of a cost-of-living adjustment (COLA).

The amount of a person's Social Security benefit is based upon how much money the individual paid into the system during the course of his or her working life. Individuals with higher lifetime earnings derive more Social Security benefits. The average earnings you received from your work during a given year are adjusted to reflect across-the-board changes to average earnings since the year you were working and to make considerations based on the rate of inflation. Therefore, if you earned $4,500 annually in 1955 and you're retiring in 2012, the value for that year's salary will be adjusted upward (somewhere close $40,000 annually) when calculating your Social Security benefits.

For example, in 2003, if a retiree had average lifetime earnings of $19,670 per year, which is considered low, he or she would receive $11,070 annually in Social Security benefits. Social Security, in this case, accounts for about 56% of the retiree's average pre-retirement income. Now consider a retiree in 2003 whose average lifetime earnings exceeded the taxable cap for Social Security, which in 2013 was $110,100. This retiree's Social Security benefit would come to about $29,020 annually, which would account for only 26 percent of this retiree's average pre-retirement income. These percentage-of-working-life-income values are known as **replacement rates**—the percentage value of one's average lifetime earnings that are replaced by Social Security benefits.

The age at which an individual 'retires' also determines the amount of Social Security benefits he or she receives. The figures in the preceding paragraph assume that our example individuals elected to receive benefits at age 66. Individuals may elect to receive benefits as early as age 62, but the amount of their benefits will be lower as a result.

Meet Steve Smith

Steve Smith is a fictional Social Security beneficiary. Steve was born in 1953, and he is currently 62. His *full retirement age* is 66. Steve currently earns about $8,000 a month from his employer ($96,000 annually), and his monthly household expenses are approximately $7,500 a month. Steve's earned enough Social Security credits over the course of his lifetime to qualify for benefits (see Chapter 5), and since he entered the workforce in 1971, his earnings have increased steadily, roughly at the rate of the national average for earnings increases.

Steve would like nothing better than to retire now (62), rather than wait for his full retirement age (66). But in order to retire, he wants to be sure that he'll have enough money coming in post-retirement to cover his monthly expenses.

Steve Waits and Retires at 66, His Full Retirement Age

Were he to wait until he reached 66, so as to receive his full benefit payment (also referred to as a *primary insurance amount*), then he would receive $2,216 from Social Security monthly ($26,592 annually). Since Steve's pre-retirement earnings are $8,000 a month, his replacement rate would be 28%. In order to fully compensate for his pre-retirement income, Steve would need to have other retirement income worth $5,784 monthly ($8,000 - $2,216) or $69,408 annually. Remember though, Steve's household expenses ($7,500/month) are $500 less monthly than his pre-retirement income ($8,000/month). In theory, Steve could get by with $6,000 ($500*12) less annually. His non-Social Security retirement income would thus need only be $63,408 ($69,408-$6,000).

Question : How is the Primary Insurance Amount Calculated?

Calculating the PIA is technically complex, yet theoretically simple. First, the amounts earned during the 35 years in which you earned the most are averaged. Before your highest earning years can be identified, however, a special index must be applied to adjust each year's earnings in relation to the average nationwide earnings for that particular year. So, if you earned **$5,000** in 1955 and are seeking Social Security benefits in 2015, your 1955 earnings are multiplied by a factor of **13.6** to give them their equivalent value in today's dollars. (**13.6** x **$5,000** = **$68,000**). The factor of 13.6 was selected from an actuarial table supplied by the Social Security Administration.

For example, fictional beneficiary, John Doe, has earned the 2015 equivalent of exactly **$68,000** during his 35 highest earning years. To calculate John's Primary Insurance Amount, first multiply **$68,000** by **35** to get **$2,380,000**. Then, divide this figure by **420** (the number of months in 35 years) to get **$5,666.67**. Round down to nearest whole dollar value, **$5,666**, and this is John Doe's 'average indexed monthly earnings'.

$$\$68,000 * 35 = \$2,380,000$$
$$\$2,380,000 / 420 \text{ months} = \$5,666.67 \approx \$5,666$$

John's average indexed monthly earnings are <u>$5,666</u>

A complex formula is then applied to the indexed monthly earnings to calculate the Primary Insurance Amount, and for those of you who enjoy that sort of thing, here's a walk-through: take **90%** of the first **$826** dollars of the average indexed monthly earnings, which is $743.40 in our example.

Next, take the average indexed monthly earnings amount (**$5,666** in this example) and take everything above $826 and less than or equal to $4,980 (in this example this equals **$4,154** ($4,980 - $826) and multiply it by **32%**, (which equals **$1,329.28**). Next, again using the average indexed monthly earnings, multiply the amount greater than $4,980 (**$686** for John Doe) by **15%**, (which is **$102.90**).

Finally, take the three products you've just calculated–$743.40, $1,329.28, and $102.90 in the example– and add them all together (**$2,175.58**) and round down to the lowest whole dollar amount: **$2,175**. $2,175 is John Doe's Primary Insurance Amount.

$$\text{Value}_1 : \$826 * .9 = \$743.40$$
$$\text{Value}_2 : \$4,980 - \$826 = \$4,154$$
$$\$4,154 * .32 = \$1,329.28$$
$$\text{Value}_3 : \$686 * .15 = \$102.90$$

$$\text{John's Primary Insurance Amount} = \textbf{Value}_1 + \textbf{Value}_2 + \textbf{Value}_3$$
$$\$743.40 + \$1{,}329.28 + \$102.90 = \$2{,}175.58 \approx \textbf{\$2{,}175}$$

John's Primary Insurance Amount is <u>$2,175</u>

The application of this formula is intended to allow lower wage earners to derive a greater proportion of their pre-retirement income from Social Security in relation to higher wage earners. Luckily, your friends at the Social Security Administration have created an online 'quick calculator' tool with which you can just plug in your salary data and automatically get your estimated Primary Insurance Amount without having to break out your calculator—*http://www.ssa.gov/OACT/quickcalc/index.html.*

Now, Steve Smith has just plain had enough of the working life and is dead set on retiring right now, at age 62. He also decides that he's going to need to receive his Social Security benefits right away, even if his monthly benefit will end up being permanently lower than his primary insurance amount of $2,216, which he would have received had he waited until his full retirement age of 66. The question then becomes:

How much less will Steve receive since he decided to retire at age 62?

To calculate Steve's benefit amount at 62, we first want to calculate the total number of months separating Steve's actual retirement from his full retirement age. If we assume roughly four full years between Steve's retiring at 62 and his 66th birthday, then we can calculate the total number of months at **48** (4 * 12). In early retirement, Social Security benefits are reduced $5/9^{\text{ths}}$ of one percent per month before the full retirement age for up to 36 months. If the beneficiary retires more than 36 months prematurely, then an additional $5/12^{\text{ths}}$ of one percent is reduced per each month over 36.

For Steve's situation, first take 5/9ths (**.556**) of one percent (.556 * .01 = .00556) of **$2,216**, his primary insurance amount. This comes to **$12.32**. Multiplying $12.32 by **48** equals **$591.36**. There are still 12 months to account for—month 37 through month 48. Take 5/12ths (**.417**) of one percent (.417 * .01=.00417) of **$2,216** to get **$9.24** and multiply it by **12** to get **$110.88**. Next add $591.36 to $110.88 to get **$702.24**, Steve's total penalty for early retirement. Subtract this amount from Steve's primary insurance amount ($2,216 - $702.24) and Steve will receive **$1,513.76** monthly from Social Security if he retires at age 62. So if Steve needs $7,500 monthly to pay for expenses, then his non-Social Security post-retirement earnings need to be at least **$5,985.64** ($7,500 - $1514.36). Retirees in situations similar to Steve's usually supplement their Social Security earnings with investment income, pensions, or employment post-retirement.

$$.00556 * \$2,216 = \$12.32$$
$$\text{Value}_1 : \$12.32 * 48 \text{ months} = \$591.36$$
$$.00417 * \$2,216 = \$9.24$$
$$\text{Value}_2 : \$9.24 * 12 = \$110.88$$

$$\text{Steve's total penalty} = \text{Value}_1 + \text{Value}_2$$
$$\$591.36 + \$110.88 = \$702.24$$

$$\text{Steve's total payment} = \text{Steve's PIA} - \text{Steve's total penalty}$$
$$\text{OR}$$
$$\$2,216 - \$702.24 = \$1,513.76$$

Steve's Total Payment = $1,513.76

Exceptions

Some individuals may have worked for a large part of their lives and not paid taxes into Social Security but instead qualified for a separate retirement pension. This situation is most common for individuals who worked for a government agency, a nonprofit organization or in another country. In accordance with a legal measure known as *The Windfall Elimination Provision* or WEP, the SSA reduces the amount of Social Security benefits awarded on the basis of how many or how few years the beneficiary has spent earning 'substantial earnings' while also paying Social Security taxes.

As was explained in detail previously in this chapter, a person's primary insurance amount is determined by separating a person's average indexed monthly earnings into multiple tiers. For everything from $0 to $826, a factor of 90% is applied. For everything from $827 and less than or equal to $4,980, a factor of 32% is applied. And for everything greater than $4,980, a factor of 15% is applied. The Windfall Elimination Provision reduces the first factor from 90% to as low as 40% in accordance with a specific index. For example, recall our John Doe from our previous technical example who had average indexed monthly earnings of $5,180. Using this figure, we originally calculated his primary insurance amount at $2,102. For the purpose of this illustration, John received earnings from 1972 to 1983 while working for the federal government, and during this time the federal government, as an employer, did not participate in Social Security.

Instead of participating in the Social Security program, the Federal Government had a separate pension set up for federal workers. In December of 1983, as part of the 1983 Social Security Amendments, Social Security was expanded to cover employees of the federal government, state and local governments, as well as non-profits. The problem arose when the workers for these employers were suddenly eligible to receive both Social Security and pension incomes. And while

John Doe would be happy to reap this windfall, it wouldn't be financially prudent for the Social Security Administration.

John went on to work for 25 more years while having Social Security taxes withheld. Assuming that John earned at levels that the SSA deemed 'substantial'—$6,675 in 1983…$19,800 in 2010… $22,050 in 2015—for a total of 25 years, then a factor of 65%, rather than 90%, would be applied to the first segment ($827 and less), during the course of calculating John's total primary insurance amount. This means that he'll still get the pension that he earned from 1972 to 1983 while working for the government, but he'll get slightly less Social Security benefits, which is only fair given that he wasn't paying into Social Security for nearly a decade of his working career. For people like John who fall under the dictates of the Windfall Elimination Provision, the fewer the years of 'substantial' earnings while incurring Social Security taxes, the lower the percentage applied to that first segment ($827 and less) of the PIA calculation.

Even though the benefit payouts of Social Security may seem modest, that assessment is based on the level of dependence many Americans have on Social Security. In 2012, approximately two out of three American Social Security beneficiaries were dependent on Social Security for half or more of their income. One in three received 90% or more of their income from Social Security. What makes this statistic particularly poignant is that Social Security has lifted 14.7 million senior citizens out of poverty. Without Social Security benefits, over 40% of Americans aged 65 and older would have incomes well below the poverty line. Social Security benefits have dramatically cut that number to just below 10%.

Minority Populations & Social Security

Social Security benefits have become of particular importance to people of color and other minorities, as they are statistically less likely to receive retirement earnings from other assets, such as IRAs, pensions and 401(k) plans. In 2010, only 30% of African Americans retirees and 19% of Hispanic retirees received retirement income from any of the aforementioned financial sources, while white Americans received 42% of their retirement income from sources other than wages and Social Security.

Among retirees in 2012, 74% of African Americans and 77 % of Hispanics depended on Social Security for half or more of their incomes, and 49% of African Americans and 55% of Hispanics depended on Social Security for 90 percent or more of their incomes. Among white retirees, 65%depended on Social Security for half or more of their incomes and 35%depended on Social Security 90% or more.

Americans of color—who on average are statistically likely to earn less than white Americans—are prone to getting more value out of Social Security in the way of easing the transition to retirement. This is because the system follows a ***progressive benefit formula***, meaning that lower-income earners have a greater portion of their pre-retirement income provided by their Social Security benefit packages. Furthermore, the Social Security disability benefit is of particular importance to the African American demographic because African Americans have statistically shown higher disability rates before the age of 65.

Social Security & Women

In 2012, 77% of unmarried women, who were unmarried because they were never married or by way of divorce or being widowed, relied on Social Security for half or more of their incomes. Forty-nine percent of these women relied on Social Security for 90% or more of their incomes. The respective figures for married couples are 53% and 23% and for unmarried men, 67% and 40%, respectively.

This makes Social Security benefits important for women, who on average earn less than their equivalent male counterparts. They also benefit disproportionately from many of the program's assistance-based aspects versus men, as women tend to have longer life expectancies.

Social Security & Pensions

As of 2012, most retired Americans do not receive pension incomes, making Social Security that much more important for them. Among retired couples, just less than half, or 48%, receive pension income. Retired Americans who are unmarried are even less likely to have pension incomes—only 34% of unmarried women and 38% of unmarried men.

These numbers of pension earners are consistent with the overall is decline of Americans who earn pensions; these numbers are expected to be substantially lower in the future than even we see today. Social Security is thus poised to play an even more pronounced role in the financial wellbeing of retired Americans. Even amongst those Americans receiving pensions, the amounts distributed through pensions are not usually set up to keep pace with the ever-rising cost of living. Social Security benefits, by contrast, have an automatic cost-of-living adjustment (COLA) built into the program.

67 is the new 65

Back in 1983, the Greenspan commission scheduled an increase of the 'full-benefit' retirement age from 65 to 67 between 2002 and 2027, and we are in the midst of this transition now. Because of this change, benefits at all ages are in the process of being decreased. Take, for instance, those Americans who choose to start taking their Social Security benefits early at age 62. Rather than receiving nearly 80% of their benefit at age 62, they will instead receive only about 70%. There's talk of extending the full retirement age to 70 at some point in the future, so millennials (individuals reaching adulthood around the year 2000) should plan for this likely eventuality.

In order to fully understand the impact of the change in the age at which full benefits are payable, it's important to understand exactly what the term 'payable benefits' entails. Depending on when you choose to start receiving payments (benefits) from Social Security, you are subject to receiving a certain percentage of your 'primary insurance amount' or PIA. Your PIA, as discussed earlier in this chapter, is a function of your average pre-retirement income. If your PIA, for instance, is $1,200 monthly ($14,400 annually), and you elect to begin receiving your benefit at your full retirement age (66) then you will receive 100% of your PIA for the rest of your life.

If you decide to take your benefit early, at age 62 for example, then you will receive about 75% of your PIA or $900 monthly ($10,800 annually) for the rest of your life. If you choose to delay receiving your benefit until you are older than 66, let's say for example age 70, then you'd received approximately 132% of your benefit amount, which is $1,584 monthly ($19,008 annually) for the rest of your life. The amount you receive is subject, however, to an ongoing cost-of-living adjustment (COLA), which ranges from 0 to 4 percent with each passing year. As a point of reference, The COLA adjustment for 2015 was 1.5%.

As the full retirement age is raised (currently 66 and soon to be 67), the entire benefits schedule adjusts upward. The full retirement age represents the baseline for receiving 100% of your Social Security benefit. The percentage that you're eligible to receive of your PIA, as determined by your early or late retirement, will always automatically scale according to the current full retirement age.

Choosing When to Receive Benefits

The initiation of your Social Security benefits can be begin anywhere from age 62 to age 70, based on the recipient's personal preference—represented by when an individual 'retires'. There are a multitude of factors to consider when deciding when to begin receiving your Social

Security benefits. A lot of relatively financially secure individuals tend to delay receiving Social Security for as long as possible so that they end up receiving a larger benefit. While this may be the best approach for certain individuals in some situations, it may not be the best option for others.

For instance, if you're closing in on age 66, and you're drawing a significant amount of your income from other retirement accounts such as an IRA or 401(k), you may be inclined to delay receiving Social Security benefits since you're capable of getting along without them. This of course means that you will also receive a bigger payout when you do eventually cash in. In this eventuality, however, you really must stop to consider whether delaying your Social Security benefit makes sense if it means more money coming out of your other retirement accounts. The interest gained on these accounts, if left intact, may prove even more lucrative than the extra social security you'll receive by waiting to take your benefit.

Meet Jeb Johnson

To illustrate, here's another fictitious retiree, Jeb Johnson. Jeb's currently aged 66, his full retirement age, and his most recent annual salary is $75,000. Since Jeb began working over 30 years ago, his income has risen steadily in accordance with the national average. Were he to begin receiving his Social Security benefits immediately, he'd receive $2,185 monthly; this is his PIA.

Jeb, however, is questioning whether he should take his benefits now. He has another major source of post-retirement income in the form of his employer-sponsored 401(k) to which he's been contributing for several decades. The 401(k) is currently worth $376,000 and it's still growing aggressively. If Jeb wants to, he can begin receiving distributions from his 401(k) immediately.

Jeb's home is paid for, and he's able to live on about $3,500 a month. He wants to travel a lot during his retirement, so he's budgeting an additional $5,000 annually for travel expenses. If Jeb distributes his travel budget and adds it to his $3,500 monthly living requirement, then he's looking at about **$3,916** that he needs to bring in monthly to meet his financial goals. His Social Security benefit would cover more than half of that, but he could just as easily withdraw the whole amount from his 401(k) minus any other post-retirement earnings he may have coming in. Furthermore, if Jeb delays receiving his Social Security until age 70, then he'll receive approximately 132% of his PIA (132% of $2,185) or **$2,884** for the rest of his life.

According to Christine Benz, the director of personal finance for Morningstar, when estimating the performance of a solid 401(k) plan, a 5% annual growth rate is reasonable to expect. Therefore, if Jeb elects to defer his Social Security and take out **$3,916** from his 401(k) every month for the next four years, then Jeb will be losing the 5% return for the money he withdraws. To make things easier to estimate, assume an annual rather than a monthly distribution:

Year 1 : Jeb is 66, and ($3,916 * 12) or **$46,992** will be withdrawn during year one. Five percent of $46,992 is **$2,349.60**. This is the amount of interest earnings that Jeb will give up by receiving distributions of this particular amount during his first year of retirement.

If Jeb elects to begin receiving Social Security at 66, then he will only need, presumably, **$1,731** withdrawn monthly from his 401(k) ($3,916 - $2,185 = $1,731). That's an annual distribution of $20,772, 5% of which is **$1,038.60**. Therefore, Jeb is going to be saving about $1,300 in interest earnings every year by receiving Social Security benefits at 66 rather than 70 – a total of about **$5,200** or ($1,300 * 4). We also have to take into account that each successive year that Jeb withdraws his full financial need from his 401(k), he'll be losing the interest earnings from previous years as well.

Year 2 : Jeb is 67. After this year Jeb will have lost two years of interest on the amount he withdrew during Year 1 in addition to the interest lost in the current year. After four years the total amount of interest earnings Jeb loses, in a scenario in which he does not receive Social Security benefits until age 70, is approximately **$23,496**.

$$\$2,349.60 * 1 = \$2,349.60$$
$$\$2,349.60 * 2 = \$4,699.20$$
$$\$2,349.60 * 3 = \$7,048.80$$
$$\$2,349.60 * 4 = \$9,398.40$$

$$\$2,349.60 + \$4,699.20 + \$7,048.80 + \$9,398.40 = \$23,496.00$$

The actual figure would be slightly higher than **$23,496** because of the growth effects of ***compound interest***.

Now, let's look at the scenario in which Jeb begins receiving his Social Security benefit at age 66 and only needs to withdraw **$1,731** monthly from his 401(k). In this scenario, Jeb won't lose quite so much in interest earnings:

$$\$1,038.60 * 1 = \$1,731$$
$$\$1,038.60 * 2 = \$2,077.20$$
$$\$1,038.60 * 3 = \$3,115.80$$
$$\$1,038.60 * 4 = \$4,154.40$$

$$\$1,731 + \$2,077.20 + \$3,115.80 + \$4,154.40 = \$10,386$$

Jeb is left with a difference of about **$13,110** in 401(k) interest earnings that he would have saved by taking his Social Security benefit at age 66. Now, Jeb would need to account for the fact that his monthly Social Security benefit payment would be larger at 70 than it would be at 66 ($2,884 vs. $2,185), a difference of **$699**. Were Jeb to delay receiving benefits until age 70 then he'd make up his 401(k) interest losses in 9 months. Therefore, Jeb is probably better off relying on his 401(k) and deferring his social security benefits.

Another circumstance that might lead you to consider taking your benefits earlier rather than later is if you're unable to find full-time work. Older workers statistically take a longer time to find new work when unemployed. According to a 2012 Pew Research Study, over 43% of workers who were unemployed for a year or longer were age 55 or older.

In some emergency situations, you may want to consider taking Social Security early, but just to get through a rough period. You don't anticipate needing the Social Security money on an indefinite basis, but just until you find a job or otherwise find yourself in a more comfortable position financially. If this is the case, then you should consider repaying the Social Security benefits you receive.

That's right, during your first year of receiving benefits, you can 'withdraw your application' and stop receiving the benefits. You will have to pay back the benefits you've received to that point, but afterwards it will be as if you never began taking benefits. This option, however, may only be exercised during the first 12 months of your 'pseudo' retirement. After you've been receiving benefits for 12 months, you cannot discontinue them.

You may also elect to take your benefits early if you're working part-time. When it comes to working while receiving your Social Security benefits, after you reach the full retirement age, you're free to earn as much as you want from employment or from a business. If you're considering taking your benefit before your full retirement age, then that's a bit of a different story.

> You may only withdraw from your benefits once per lifetime. All benefits must be paid back including those that were received by your spouse and/or children.

As of 2014, persons taking an early Social Security payment are allowed to earn up to $15,480 annually without having to sacrifice any of their Social Security benefits. Upon reaching this earnings threshold, Social Security benefits are reduced by $1 for every extra $2 earned beyond the $15,480 threshold. Things change slightly during the year in which you reach full retirement age. During this year, you can earn up to $3,450 a month in the months prior to your birthday. If you earn more than this monthly cap, then you will lose $1 in benefits for every $3 you earn above the cap. Generally speaking, it doesn't make good financial sense to take Social Security if you're earning an income above the threshold, but some extenuating circumstances can warrant such a strategy.

Meet Gus Mendez

Gus Mendez, another fictitious retiree, has dreamed for years of writing the next great American novel, but between his work and family obligations, he's been unable to put together the time to do so. His kids have left the nest, and he's asked his boss to go from full-time to part-time at work so that he can pursue his literary ambitions. Gus' income has subsequently decreased from $4,750 monthly to $2,917 monthly.

Unfortunately, Gus' savings were eaten up by high college tuition costs and a messy divorce. The 2008 financial collapse catastrophically destroyed what was left. Gus is accustomed to living on his full-time salary, and he's interested in using Social Security to help him supplement his newly part-time income. If he plays his cards right, Gus thinks he can cut down his monthly expenditures to about $4,250.

Gus has just turned 62. His full retirement age is 66. Gus has earned enough Social Security Credits to begin receiving benefits (see Chapter 5), and if he elects to receive Social Security now, he will be entitled to receive $1,130 monthly. Add that to his part-time salary and Gus will almost be at $4,250 in monthly income.

However, there's a problem. A friend at the grocery store where Gus works informed him that there are penalties for individuals who receive Social Security early while continuing to work. Gus does some research and learns about the $15,480 threshold. He will be penalized a dollar for every $2 he earns above this threshold, and he's concerned as to whether or not he'll still be able to meet his monthly expenditures after the penalty is levied.

Since Gus' salary is **$2,917** monthly or **$35,000** a year, **$19,520** worth of earnings will be penalized. Gus would like to find out at exactly what point in the year his benefits will begin to be reduced. He would thus need to figure out how long it takes him to earn $15,480. One quick way to do this is to express **$15,480** as a percentage of Gus' annual salary—**$15,840 / $35,000 = .4423** or **44.2%**. Next, he needs to figure out 44.2% of a 12-month calendar year—**44.2% * 12 = 5.3 = 3/10ths of the way into the month of May.**

Therefore, it would be somewhere in the 2nd week of May that Gus would break the $15,480 threshold and see the reduction in his Social Security benefits. Every week after the threshold is met, Gus' benefits will reduced by about $336.25. His weekly pay with a **$35,000** salary would be about **$673.08** ($35,000/52), and for every two dollars earned ($673.08/2), he'll be penalized one dollar (**$336.54 in total per week**). It would only be three and a half weeks (about the first week of June) before Gus would no longer have any Social Security benefits coming in. When Gus realizes that he won't be able to both work and depend on Social Security to supplement his working income, he decides get a literary agent and get an advance payment for his sure-to-be amazing novel in progress.

Gus' situation is a common situation bound to play out when individuals attempt to hang onto their salaries while collecting Social Security before their full retirement age. Gus has to take into account that even after he reaches full retirement age, his benefit amount would have remained at $1,130 permanently, which is considerably lower than it would be had he waited until his full retirement age. Also, it's worth considering that if Gus waits until his full retirement age, then he will be free to work as much as he wants without penalty. Some individuals choose to receive benefits early because, even though they have more than adequate incomes through wages or other retirement earnings, they're interested in transferring their financial assets to someone else. These individuals may begin taking benefits early for the purpose of investing the money into a trust fund or in stocks to benefit their chosen beneficiaries. Another reason someone may want to take his Social Security benefits early is if he is looking to invest in something particular, like a boat or an RV. Doing this is fine if he's got an adequate retirement plan in place.

In the event that benefits recipient passes away, her benefits will legally transfer to her spouse if the spouse's benefits are lower than her own. Social Security recipients are unable to confer their post-mortem Social Security earnings at-will. This is why early receipt of Social Security benefits may be attractive to those looking to transfer financial assets to another party. Chapter 3 will include a deeper discussion on smart approaches to Social Security for couples.

Finally, it behooves a Social Security recipient to consider how long he or she expects to live. A heavy smoker whose parents both died in their early seventies may do better taking what he can get when he can get it. Should you need someone to consult with you about your life expectancy, you can find resources through AARP (American Association of Retired Persons) or T. Rowe Price to help you evaluate your expected benefits within the context of your expected lifespan. It's a little easier to decide when you should enroll in Social Security's healthcare offshoot, Medicare. Under most any circumstances, you should enroll in Medicare as soon as you first become eligible at age 65. Failing to do so may subject you to higher premiums in the future.

A Word to the Wealthy

Since only a certain quantity of income can be subject to Social Security withholdings ($118,500 in 2015), very wealthy individuals may only receive so much in benefits— $2,663 monthly if initiating benefits at the full retirement age in 2015, $3,501 if initiating benefits at age 70 in 2015. Every year, the maximum taxable amount of income increases slightly. In 2017, it is projected to reach $126,300 and in 2019 it is projected to have reached $139,800.

Dr. Paul, our newest fictional retiree to join the group, has been practicing geriatric medicine for nearly four decades and has, for the majority of this time, earned a salary that exceeded the maximum taxable amount for Social Security. He's put as much money into the system as is possible to put into it—at least by any one individual. Dr. Paul is retiring at age 66. He doesn't need any additional income, but he's not sure whether he has anything to gain by delaying receipt of his Social Security benefit. Dr. Paul thinks he may have 'maxed out' and that he'll receive essentially the same distribution amount at 70 as he'd receive if he elects to take his benefit now at 66. He knows that if he begins receiving his benefit now he'll receive **$2,663** a month.

Fortunately, Dr. Paul has a good financial advisor and is soon made aware that even though he is a lifelong high-income earner, he'll still receive a substantially larger Social Security benefit if he waits until age 70 to file. Dr. Paul will be 70 in 2019, at which point the primary insurance amount derived from Dr. Paul's contributions will have risen slightly to **$2,708**. And since Dr. Paul will have delayed receipt of benefits for four years, he'll be entitled to the same **132%** increase in his benefit amount as would any other 70-year-old first time Social Security recipient. Dr. Paul will thus receive, beginning at 70 years old, a distribution of **$3,575** (132% * $2,708) every month for the rest of his life.

| 2 |

Avoilding Traps & Maximizing Benefits

While different strategies will work for different people based on their situation, it can be beneficial to know what your options will be and what the experiences of others can teach us about the smartest way to use your Social Security benefits.

Reasons to be Skeptical

Though, as discussed in Chapter 1, there are times when electing to take your benefits before your full retirement date makes sense, make sure that you take a long, sober look at your situation before doing so. A study released by the Nationwide Financial Retirement Institute in June of 2014 found that 38% of retirees regretted taking their benefits early.

Generally speaking, members of the Social Security Administration don't give retirees seeking assistance case-by-case advice, rather they answer questions regarding policy and guidelines. This means that many people do their retirement planning and Social Security benefits process on their own or with the aid of a financial planner. The world of retirement planning can be overwhelming for many Americans, especially considering how important it is to get things right the first time. The first step to protecting yourself is picking up this book. Once armed with the necessary knowledge, you can make much more informed decisions on your own. The second step—if you do elect to use a financial planner—is to ensure that the firm you select is reputable and well-credentialed.

Be extremely cautious when investigating sales pitches that advertise exotic methodologies that will help you make thousands of dollars more from your Social Security benefits. Seniors are often the primary targets for scams and many times these 'make more from your benefits' pitches are attempts to acquire your private information. To avoid scams of this nature:

- Never give out your personal information over the telephone.

- Don't accept pre-paid debit or credit cards in someone else's name.

- Don't agree to wire money to someone you don't know. Don't fill out personal information fields on websites that are not secured or sponsored by the government.

- If someone contacts you claiming to be from the Social Security Administration, *DO NOT* give them your Social Security number or any other information until you contact the SSA yourself to verify the request.

In the event you believe you are the victim of a scam, you should report the incident to the Federal Trade Commission. You can file a report at *www.ftc.gov/idtheft* or by calling 1-877-ID-THEFT. Some of the sales pitches you encounter may not be from malicious identity thieves but may just be from fly-by-night consultants with less-than-reputable credentials who want to advise you on when and how to begin taking your benefits. Any claims from these individuals regarding the discovery of a 'weird' or 'exotic' method for helping you get the most out your benefits is disingenuous. The methods taught by these salesmen are not rocket science, and you don't need a so-called 'consultant' to perform them.

For example, the ***file and suspend*** rule is a so-called tactic that, though slightly complicated, is something you should be able to figure out on your own. The file and suspend option was added to Social Security in conjunction with the Senior Citizen's Freedom to Work Act. The file and suspend provision allows for one party in a couple to file for benefits and immediately defer these benefits, allowing them to accumulate deferred payment credits of up to 8 percent per year. Meanwhile the beneficiary's spouse can immediately begin collecting his or her spousal benefits even though the beneficiary's Social Security payments are suspended. We'll do a step-by-step walk-through of the file and suspend strategy in Chapter 3.

If You're Single

Being a single person makes the Social Security picture a little simpler. Since you don't have to worry about the benefits your spouse will receive if you die, all you need to know is that your benefits—to put it bluntly—are going to expire when you do. Because single individuals need only concern themselves with their own personal financial well-being, there's generally less of an incentive amongst this demographic to defer receiving their benefits until after they've surpassed full retirement age.

Single individuals who are self-sufficient financially, by way of a good paycheck or other retirement benefits, should still file at age 66 and request that their benefits be suspended. This means essentially that a 66-year-old, financially self-sufficient individual should claim his retirement earnings at age 66, meaning he's due to receive his full PIA (Primary Insurance Amount), but he should then elect to suspend payment on these benefits until a later time after they've presumably accumulated some delayed-retirement credits. This is different from choosing not to file a claim until after exceeding his full retirement age. Though waiting to file until later will result in a monthly/yearly benefit amount larger than his PIA, if he or she dies or faces a catastrophic injury or sickness before such a time, Social Security will be of little use. If the single individual files at 66 and suspends payment, however, then the money that person is earning (but not receiving) is available to him or her whenever it is eventually needed.

Social Security will not pay retroactive benefits for any months prior to the point at which you reach the full retirement age. So, if you decide at 65 that you really need a nice cash windfall, and you ask to receive the payout you would have received had you filed at 63, then you won't have any success. But if you've filed your claim at 66 and suspend the payments, then decide at 68 that you really need the cash to help pay for an unexpected medical issue or other costly incident, then you will be entitled to receive the benefit amount that's been accumulating since your 66th birthday, paid retroactively in full. Generally, the flexibility of the file and suspend option for singles makes it more attractive and more useful than delaying your claim outright in hopes of an overall larger benefit amount.

Maybe you're a fairly healthy individual who loves his or her job, and who really just doesn't feel like getting involved with Social Security at the moment but still wants to make smart financial decisions. When crunching the numbers to determine whether you want to delay filing or to file and then postpone your benefits, remember that every year that goes by, your benefit increases by about 8 percent. But if you wait to file and end up needing a quick cash influx, then you'll regret not taking advantage of the file and suspend option.

Meet Mark Mettcalf

Meet Mark Mettcalf, another fictional retiree, though he's not really a retiree... at least not yet. Mark's always dreamed of owning a little donut shop in his hometown of Whistlewood, North Carolina. He's spent his career working as a foreman for a construction company, but he's now 66 years old and entitled to start receiving a Social Security benefit of $1,917.

Mark decides to go ahead and file for Social Security at 66 but suspend his payments. He's just received a loan from a bank and is now able to purchase a storefront for his up-and-coming donut shop. The store gets off to a booming start, and he's enormously profitable within the first two years. A regular customer tells Mark that he thinks a donut shop like his would flourish in the nearby town of Windy Hills. Mark does some research and determines that he can use some of his profits from the original donut shop to make a down payment on the storefront in Windy Hills, but he's going to be short by about $25,000, meanwhile, he'll need to hire a manager onsite to be in charge.

Mark could go back to the bank that provided his first loan, but he'd prefer to open up the Windy Hills shop without incurring any more debt. Since he suspended his Social Security payments at age 66, Mark, now age 68, is entitled to receive his deferred Social Security payments in one lump sum. Since each of the previous years' accumulated payments have earned an 8% delayed payment credit, they are now worth about $7,500. Mark decides to cash in on his suspended payments to finance his new Windy Hills shop. From this point forward, Mark will also receive his primary insurance amount $1,917 every month as well.

Work-arounds

Though, as mentioned in Chapter 2, if you're receiving Social Security benefits before the full retirement age and you're also working, you lose a dollar in benefits for every two dollars you make over the earning limit, which in 2015 is $15,720. It is for this reason that financial planners often caution against taking Social Security benefits early if you're earning a substantial amount of income from working. That said, the money you lose from earning above the earning limit is not lost forever.

Once you reach full retirement age, your benefits are refigured to take into account how much of your benefits were lost as a result of your excess earning. For example, let's say you claim your benefits at age 63, and over the next three years you lose the equivalent of one full year's worth of benefits due to exceeding the earnings threshold. When you reach full retirement age (66), then these earning are returned in the form of a higher benefit. Your benefits are paid out as if you'd started taking benefits two (instead of three) years prior to your full retirement age.

You'd still receive less benefits over the course of your entire retirement than you would have received had you never exceeded the earnings limit, and you'd certainly receive less than you would have received had you waited until your full retirement age to begin taking benefits. Remember, once you reach full retirement age, you're free to take Social Security while earning as much as you like free of any repercussions.

fig.4

Maximizing Your Benefits			
FRA	Your FRA is your Full Retirement Age	Many retirees who take their benefits early (before their FRA) regret it	
Don't Become A Victim	*Never* give out personal information to retirement planning salesman	Don't accept a pre-paid debit card in someone elses name	
	If you believe you have been the victim of identity theft, call 1-877-ID-THEFT	Verify all requests for personal information such as your Social Security number from persons claiming to represent the Social Security Administration	
Couples That File	Leveraging the file and suspend clause can allow one spouse to file but suspend the receipt of benefits while the other collects a spousal benefit. File and suspend as a benefits-maximizing tactic is covered in Chapter 3		
For Single Filings	Your benefits, once activated, are for life	You will receive higher benefits payments by waiting until your FRA	Your payments will be even higher the longer you wait to file
For Working Retirees	Your benefits are adjusted to account for the excess amount of money you made as a result of working past the time when you filed for Social Security		If you are earning a substantial paycheck into your retirement, postpone filing to maximize your benefit

| 3 |

What Couples Should Know

Couples have a fair degree of maneuverability when it comes to taking their Social Security entitlements. Multiple provisions are set up to ensure that spouses—who may not have been the primary breadwinner for their family, or may not have worked at all—can receive a Social Security benefit based on the benefit amount of their significant others. Provisions are also in place for a 'survival benefit' for spouses to use in the event that the primary beneficiary dies before the spouse. We'll take a look at each of these provisions along with some other key Social Security related considerations that couples face when planning their retirements.

The Spousal Benefit

The spousal benefit entitles a person to earn a Social Security benefit worth at least half as much as his or her spouse's benefit is worth. If Martha and John are married and John is the primary breadwinner for the family, his Social Security benefit is worth $3,000/month and Martha's is worth $1,000/month then Martha will receive an additional $500 monthly as a spousal benefit which brings the total household Social Security income to $4,500 monthly.

If Martha's Social Security benefit exceeds half the value of John's, then no spousal benefit is given. Just like regular Social Security benefits, if the beneficiary elects to receive benefits before his full retirement age, then those benefits will be reduced. If the beneficiary delays filing for the benefits until after she surpasses her full retirement age, then she'll receive higher monthly payments when she does file (up to 8 percent more if she waits until age 70).

Divorce

Even if the couple has divorced, the person with the smaller benefit is still entitled to 50 percent of the value of his or her spouse's benefit from Social Security, so long as the couple was married for at least 10 years. In order for a divorcée to receive the benefit, he or she must be 62 years old or older and single.

If this is the situation in which you find yourself, then you may contact the Social Security Administration directly to file your claim—you need not notify your ex. When you take a benefit on the basis of your ex's earnings record, your ex will not find out unless you tell him or her. Your claim has no effect on any claim your ex makes with regard to Social Security. Taking a spousal benefit as a divorced person is slightly different from taking the benefit while still married, because you don't even need to wait for your ex to file for his or her benefits in order to file for your own. So long as you have been divorced for at least two years, you can take your own benefit using your ex's work record, regardless of whether he or she has filed any claims with Social Security.

The Survivor Benefit

The Survivor Benefit allows you to receive the full amount of your partner's Social Security benefit after his or her death; assuming of course, that your personal Social Security entitlement is less than your spouse's. If you have a larger Social Security benefit than your spouse, then you will want to be very careful about when you begin receiving benefits. If you elect to receive benefits before your full retirement age (meaning that your payouts will be lower for the duration of your lifetime) your spouse will receive a smaller payout than he or she'd receive had you waited until you reached or exceeded your full retirement age.

Every couple will have to sort through the details of the unique situation that faces each of them. They will need to assess many variables such as how much larger one benefit will be in relation to another and the average life expectancies of both parties. Take for example another fictional couple—Beth and Greg. Beth is four years younger than Greg, and she's likely to outlive him by 6-8 years. Beth's personal Social Security and other retirement benefits will not account for much relative to Greg's, so Greg decides to wait until age 70 to claim his Social Security retirement benefits. By doing this, he ensures that Beth's survival benefit will be substantial—equal to Greg's retirement benefit taken 4 years after his full retirement age (FRA). Meanwhile, if they need a bit of extra cash, Beth can begin receiving her own benefit early. This approach certainly limits the amount of benefits received in the short-term, but is a very conservative and responsible approach to the likely longer-term realities.

File & Suspend

Another strategy often employed by couples is the file and suspend technique, mentioned briefly in Chapter 2. If Greg and Beth were to use this technique, Greg would file at his full retirement age of 66 instead of waiting until he reached age 70. He would then elect to suspend payments on his benefits. Meanwhile, since Greg has technically filed his Social Security claim, Beth is now allowed to file for spousal benefits (worth ½ of Greg's benefits) so long as she is at least 62 years old, even though Greg is not actually receiving payments. If Greg and Beth both live late into their eighties, the file and suspend method can increase the total value of their Social Security payments by over 10 percent.

The file and suspend strategy works best when the higher earning spouse wants to keep working late into his or her sixties, and the lower earning spouse is looking to retire but wants to do so with a more substantial benefit to replace the missing income.

If you attempt the file and suspend strategy and then change your mind, deciding that you would prefer instead to receive your benefits, then you can do so fairly easily. Social Security allows those who've

Only one member of a couple may file and suspend, not both. It is not permitted for both spouses in a couple to simultaneously take the spousal benefit off of the other's Social Security benefit.

suspended their benefits to access an 'escape hatch' whereby the benefits they've suspended are immediately issued to them. This can happen by way of a lump sum payment or by adjusting the individual's monthly distribution amount upward to account for the funds that have been suspended. For an example of the latter approach, if you've had a year's worth of benefit payments suspended, then you can opt to start your 68th year with the same benefit payout you'd have received had you waited until 68 to file (not just collect) your benefits.

In the event you or your spouse decides to suspend benefits, there is no formal process for doing so. The proper way to request a suspension in benefit payments is by making the request orally (over the phone) or by writing your request and sending it in the mail to the Social Security Administration.

Taking a Temporary Spousal Benefit

The 'temporary spousal benefit' is not a formal term but an arbitrary name for a Social Security strategy that works for a lot of couples. Let's say that Greg is 66 (his FRA) and set to receive $2,000 per month in Social Security. Beth is 62 and makes less than Greg. She is set to collect $1,000 monthly when she reaches age 66 (her FRA). If she decides to take her retirement now, she will only receive $750/month since she hasn't yet reached her FRA.

Greg may decide that, rather than beginning to take his $2,000 per month, he'd rather claim his spousal benefit, which is worth $500 per month.

So even though Greg's income greatly exceeds Beth's, and even though Beth has not even made it yet to full retirement age, Greg can still claim a spousal benefit reflecting Beth's anticipated FRA amount.

So while Greg awaits his 70th birthday (four years away), the couple is taking in $1,250 in Social Security retirement benefits. After four years, Greg will take his own Social Security benefit, now worth $2,640, since he waited until four years after his FRA. The couple's

Greg's spousal benefit is determined by his wife's full FRA benefit amount, not the benefit amount she'd receive if she decided to take Social Security at 62 ($750/month).

total retirement benefit is now worth $3,390 monthly until one of them dies. At which point the survivor will be receiving $2,640, which is not a bad deal (all things considered).

In these various example strategies for couples, one common thread that connects each scenario is the practice of having at least one member of the couple wait until the full retirement age or older to take his or her benefit. Retired couples will fare better in the long run when they work from positions of strength and cooperation rather than desperation or greed.

The only major risk that couples that elect to implement one of these strategies face is the risk that one of the two might die before the bulk of the benefits kick in. Therefore, if one of the spouses is facing a significant health threat, he or she may want to consider taking more benefits earlier than would be advantageous to take in the event that both spouses were in good health.

Chapter Recap

fig.5

What Couples Should Know About Social Security			
The Spousal Benefit	Entitles a person to earn a SS benefit worth at least half of that of their spouse	If the spouse's benefit exceeds half then no spousal benefit is given	
Divorce	Divorcée is entitled to 50% the value of spouse's SS benefit	The couple must have been married at least 10 years	The couple must be divorced at least 2 years
The Survivor Benefit	Allows one partner to receive his/her partner's benefit after the partner's death	Often best for individuals with lower benefits than their partners	
File & Suspend	Allows the spouse with a lower benefit to collect against his/her spouse's filing	The spouse with the higher benefit files but suspends receipt of benefit payments	Only one member of a couple can file and suspend– not both

| 4 |

How Taxes Affect Social Security

During its early decades, Social Security income was completely tax exempt under the rationale that the benefits income was derived from wages that were subject to taxation once already. It would thus be unfair to tax those wages again in the form of Social Security benefits. According to this line of thought, Social Security income was considered 'after tax' income.

The federal government's attitude towards taxing Social Security benefits has changed over time. One piece of evidence supporting the rationale for Social Security taxation comes from an analysis of Social Security's private sector counterpart, private pensions. The actual worker earnings that go into a pension fund are already taxed up-front, so when those earnings are recovered years later in the form of pension payouts, they are not taxed. But what a retiree pulls out of a pension is both the worker's earnings and the added value brought about by the pension's maturity, and with most pensions, this latter component of the pension payout is indeed taxable as it was accrued tax free.

The SSA claims that only 15% of the Social Security benefits being paid out come from the already once-taxed payroll taxes, with the other 85% of the benefits coming from other largely untaxed sources. This is the philosophical justification for the reason why Social Security benefits should be subject to some taxation. Long story short, since the time your paycheck first contributed a fraction of its dollars and cents to FICA, those dollars and cents have expanded in value, and that expansion has been largely untaxed.

The Social Security Advisory Council was formed in the 1970's to evaluate the future financing of the program. The suggestion of taxing some of the benefits payable by Social Security rose from this council. In the early 80's the Greenspan Commission made a specific recommendation that an income threshold be established, and that 50% of Social Security benefits would be taxed only after that threshold was breached. In 1983, the Greenspan Commission's recommendations found their way into law in the form of the 1983 Social Security Amendments. The thresholds were set at $25,000 for single filers and $32,000 for joint filers. A second tier of taxation was then added a decade later, mandating that individuals with income in excess of $34,000 a year and couples with income in excess of $44,000 have up to 85 percent of their Social Security income taxed.

Today, some individuals' or couples' Social Security earnings are taxable, but usually this only occurs if there is a lot of extra income coming into the household from other sources, such as wages, self-employment, or interest and dividends from investments.

As a rule, no one pays taxes on more than 85% of his or her Social Security earnings. Individuals with a combined income of between $25,000 and $34,000 still pay taxes on up to 50% of their Social Security benefits, and individuals earning more than $34,000 may see up to 85 percent of their Social Security earnings taxed. Neither of the taxation levels for joint filers have changed since the 80's, with combined household incomes between $32,000 and $44,000 subject to having 50% of their benefits taxed, and combined incomes greater than $44,000 subject to 85%.

If you are receiving Social Security benefits, then you receive a Form SSA - 1099 (also known as a Benefit Statement) every January showing how much you received in Social Security benefits the previous year.

There are a few ways to lower the amount of your Social Security benefits that is subject to tax. The most straightforward approach is to simply reduce your taxable income. If you're getting a lot of your income from withdrawals from your 401(k) or your IRA, then consider rolling these investments into a Roth IRA. Roth IRA income is not taxable and thus cannot contribute to your to your overall tax liability. To learn more about Roth IRAs, check out the Supplement at the end of this book.

Another strategy you can use is to take more out of your traditional IRA and/or 401(k) (i.e. your taxable retirement income accounts) before you begin taking Social Security benefits. So long as you're taking Social Security benefits while drawing down your taxable retirement accounts, your overall taxable income is more likely to break the thresholds, resulting in your benefits being taxed.

If there's no way to avoid breaking the income thresholds, then you can always elect to have the federal government withhold taxes from your benefits up front. You can request this type of withholding by filling out an IRS form W-4V. Your options for withholding include having 7, 10, 15 or 25 percent of your benefits payments withheld.

It's also wise to know which states are more likely to tax Social Security benefits at the state level. A study conducted by a tax and accounting firm called Wolters Kluwer found that—at time of publication—14 states will tax Social Security payments for retirees, including Colorado, North Dakota, Iowa, Kansas, Connecticut, Nebraska, New Mexico, New Jersey, Minnesota, Missouri, Montana, Rhode Island, Vermont and West Virginia.

Chapter Recap

fig.6

How Taxes Affect Social Security			
Taxable Thresholds	Social Security Amendments set thresholds to determine what levels of SS benefits would be taxed	Individuals who earn more than $25,000 and couples that earn more than $32,000 will be taxed up to 50%	Individuals who earn more than $34,000 and couples that earn more than $44,000 will be taxed up to 85%
Statements of Benefits	Form SSA – 1099 is a benefits statement	Beneficiaries receive this form every January—it shows the amount of benefits earned in the previous year	
Ways to Lower the Taxes on Your Benefits	Reduce your taxable income	Your taxable income can be reduced by rolling your 401(k) and IRA accounts into a tax-exempt Roth IRA	
	Draw more money out of your 401(k) and/or IRA accounts *before* filing for you SS benefit		Alternatively you can request to have your taxes withheld from your benefits

| 5 |

Social Security Credits

Credits are the fundamental building blocks of the Social Security program. They are earned through working and paying Social Security taxes and they are used to determine a worker's eligibility for benefits.

The use of credits has been with the Social Security system for many decades. Before 1978, the accrual of credits was determined on a quarterly basis. Individuals who earned more than $50 over the course of a 3-month calendar quarter were issued a 'quarter credit' or QC credit. Though credits are now earned on an annual basis, the same four credits per year ratio has remained intact.

In 2015, the maximum number of credits you can earn annually is 4. To earn four credits your required annual earnings must be at least $4,880. One Social Security credit is awarded per $1,220 earned during the course of the year. Every year, the amount of earnings required per credit earned increases slightly to reflect the overall increase in earnings levels.

Once a credit is earned, it is permanently affixed to your Social Security record, regardless of whether or not you continue working. For some types of workers, special rules are used to determine how credits are earned. For example, domestic workers, farm workers, and workers employed by a church or a church-affiliated organization that doesn't pay Social Security taxes are subject to such special rules.

> Credits are not earned from the receipt of income from pensions or interest or dividends from investments, but earned solely from payroll-based income.

Credits are used as a simple litmus test to determine whether or not a person is eligible to begin receiving various types of benefits. This is distinct from determining the amount of benefits to be received. For example, in the case of retirement benefits, an individual's average pre-retirement earnings and ensuing Social Security contributions determine the amount received. Raw, credit-based eligibility follows a much simpler formula.

Credits Required for Retirement Benefits

In order to be eligible for retirement benefits, an individual born in 1929 or afterwards must have worked for 10 years and accumulated 40 credits. For individuals born before 1929, not as many credits are required.

Disability Benefits

Figuring the requisite number of credits required to be eligible for disability benefits is a bit more complicated. It depends on when you became disabled and your age.

People who become disabled before the age of 24 can establish benefits eligibility with 6 credits, provided they were earned in the three-year period immediately preceding the onset of the disability. People who become disabled between the ages of 24 and 31 are awarded eligibility if they've earned credits for at least half the years between age 21 and the onset of the disability. For example, if a person became fully disabled at age 30, then she would be eligible for benefits providing she'd accumulated at least 18 Social Security credits (4.5 years of work). For persons 31 years of age or older, generally at least 20 credits are required to attain eligibility for disability benefits, and they must have been obtained in the 10 years prior to becoming disabled.

For those who are considering applying for disability benefits, keep in mind that the process is much more successful with the assistance of a professional advisor or a lawyer who specializes in Social Security Disability Insurance (SSDI). An applicant can retain representation from the very beginning of the application process but, more commonly than not, applicants try to go it alone and the process is unnecessarily lengthened by an initial denial. Once they have been rejected once, many people then elect to retain representation though doing so in the first place would have saved time and effort.

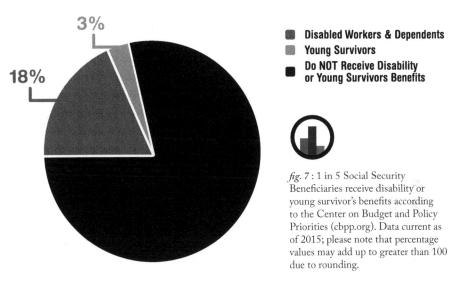

3%

18%

- Disabled Workers & Dependents
- Young Survivors
- Do NOT Receive Disability or Young Survivors Benefits

fig. 7 : 1 in 5 Social Security Beneficiaries receive disability or young survivor's benefits according to the Center on Budget and Policy Priorities (cbpp.org). Data current as of 2015; please note that percentage values may add up to greater than 100 due to rounding.

Survivor Benefits

Credits are also used to determine the eligibility of your spouse or and children in the event you die unexpectedly. The number of credits needed is determined by the age at which you die. Fewer credits are needed for those who die at an earlier age, and no one is required to have more than 40 credits in order to qualify for this benefit.

Another special provision allows or the payment of benefits to the spouse and children of the deceased even if she did not have the total requisite number of credits required. This provision can be utilized if the deceased has acquired 6 credits (one and a half years' worth of work) in the three years immediately preceding her death. For persons who die while receiving Social Security retirement benefits or disability benefits, credits need not be used to determine eligibility for survivor benefits.

Benefits instead will be paid on the basis of the specific provisions attached to the current retirement or disability entitlement.

There's No Extra Credit for Extra Credits

Most workers will end up earning many more credits than needed to qualify for the benefits they need. Unfortunately, regardless of how many credits you earn, your benefit amount does not change but is instead factored based on other methods, such as the average of your total lifetime earnings.

Chapter Recap

fig.8

Social Security Credits		
What are Social Security Credits?	Credits are earned by working. They determine an individual's eligibility to receive SS benefits	Up to four credits may be earned per year—one per each $1,220 earned—for a total of $4,880 annually
	The aforementioned dollar amounts needed to earn credits will change frequently to reflect inflation and normal rises in wages	Credits are used to determine SS benefit *eligibility*, not the amount of money they receive
How Many Credits do You Need?	For individuals born in 1929 and after they must have worked for a minimum of 10 years and accumulated at least 40 credits to earn retirement benefits	
What about Disability Benefits?	For those disabled before the age of 24 can establish eligibility with 6 credits earned within three years	For those disabled between the ages of 24 and 31 they must have earned credits for at least half the years between age 21 and the onset of the disability	For those disabled and aged over 31 years of age 20 credits are necessary for work completed fort least 10 years

Survivor Benefits	The number of credits needed is scaled to the length of your life in the event of your death	A special provision allows for the payment of benefits to the spouse and children of a beneficiary as long as they had acquired a minimum of 6 credits within the three years preceding their death.
What About Excess Credits?	There are no additional benefits given to individuals who have accumulated more than the minimum number of required Social Security Credits	

| 6 |

Applying for Benefits

If you're reading this book as part of your retirement planning, then great, you've taken the first step in getting your retirement under control. If you're reading it and retirement is just around the corner, then this chapter is for you. Applying online for Social Security benefits is easy, but the Social Security Association has some established guidelines. You may only apply online for retirement benefits or benefits as a spouse if:

- You are at least 61 years and 9 months old.
- You are not currently receiving benefits on your Social Security record.
- You have not already applied for retirement benefits.
- You want benefits to start no more than four months in the future.

The Social Security Administration will not process your application if it is made more than four months in advance. Once your application is complete, it generally takes three to four months before your first benefits deposit arrives in your bank account. This means that if your bank account changes—such as in the event of a bank merger or a compromise of your account—the SSA should be at the top of your list of parties to notify of the change.

In an effort to reduce workload and costs, local offices put a high level of emphasis on the online application. If you have a special consideration, visit _http://www.ssa.gov/_ and select 'Social Security Office Locator'. Provide some basic location information, and the site will in turn provide you with the closest office, its hours, phone number and directions.

The online system is great for the bulk of Social Security recipients and applicants, but there are some instances in which an individual may *not* apply online. For those attempting to report a death or apply for survivor's benefits, the process cannot be completed online. Furthermore, it is important to note that in many cases the funeral home reports the death to the SSA, so more often than not it is not necessary to report the death of a family member on your own; just ensure that you provide the deceased's Social Security number to the funeral home for reporting purposes.

The reporting and filing process should begin as soon as possible (if you plan to file). Because reporting cannot be done online, use the Social Security Office Locator to locate a physical office, or call 1-800-772-1213 for more information from the SSA.

If you would like to learn more about the Social Security application process, you can check out a brochure produced by the Social Security office entitled SSA Pub. No. 05-10522 or Retire Online.

Can't Handle Your Own Application?

A form SSA-11-BK must be submitted when a spouse, relative, friend, or trustee wants to manage an individual's Social Security benefit when—for whatever demonstrable reason—that individual cannot do so himself. This process is subject to approval, and in this instance the Social Security Administration does not recognize power of attorney when considering a request. If you are approved as a payee, there are some guidelines:

- You must keep an accurate record of expenses.
- You must provide an accounting of the funds taken and disbursed upon request from the SSA.
- You cannot charge a fee as a representative of a payee.

A Brief Note on FRA

Throughout the examples in this book we have used 66 as an easy FRA, and in many cases that is correct, but there are some very specific stipulations to an individual's full retirement age shown in the chart below. Remember that you can apply for benefits at age 62, but you are penalized for early filing. Keep these specific full retirement age denominations in mind when applying.

Age to Receive Full Social Security Benefits	
Year of Birth	*Full Retirement Age*
1943 – 1954	66
1955	66 and 2 months
1956	66 and 4 months
1957	66 and 6 months
1958	66 and 8 months
1959	66 and 10 months
1960 and later	67
Note: Persons born January 1st of any year should refer to the previous year	

fig. 9 : Source: *http://www.ssa.gov/pubs/EN-05-10035.pdf*

What about Same-Sex Couples?

On June 26th 2015 the US Supreme Court made a ruling in the case of Obergefell vs. Hodges mandating that same-sex couples have the right to marry in all 50 states. At the time of publication, the SSA is still updating its website and application process to reflect that many more same-sex couples are legally married and eligible for Social Security benefits.

Together with the US Department of Justice, a streamlined and comprehensive online application system is being developed, but in the meantime, same-sex couples can contact the SSA at their toll-free number 1-800-772-1213 for more information regarding the application process.

What if I am a Veteran?

Veterans applying for disability benefits should know that both the VA and SSA provide disability benefits, though the application processes and coverages are different. Furthermore, acceptance into the VA's 100% Permanent and Total program does not guarantee acceptance into the Social Security disability insurance program. There is, however, an expedited program for veterans who are applying for Social Security disability insurance. When applying—whether in person, online, or via phone—identify yourself as a veteran rated 100% P&T and be prepared to produce a copy of your VA notification of the aforementioned criteria. While this process is expedited, it may still take some time based on the nature of your disability.

Social Security & Incarceration

The laws surrounding the payment of benefits to persons who are incarcerated prohibit most forms of payment, or allow provisions for the suspension of payment if the person is incarcerated for more than 30 days.

Otherwise, as long as the individual has worked enough to earn the requisite number of SS credits and is not currently incarcerated, then he or she is still (in most cases) eligible for retirement benefits or disability benefits.

US Citizens Who Work Outside the US?

The United States has Social Security agreements with over 25 countries listed in the following table. These agreements are designed to improve benefit protection for workers who have divided their careers between the US and another country. Because of the specific nature of each of the treaties, there is not a single, governing policy. If you have questions regarding your international career, call or visit a Social Security office in the US or visit *http://www.ssa.gov/foreign/index.html* to learn about SSA resources outside of the US.

Countries with Which the US has Social Security Agreements

Australia	France	Portugal
Czech Republic	Italy	Belgium
Greece	Netherlands	Finland
South Korea	Spain	Ireland
Poland	Chile	Mexico
Switzerland	Germany	Slovak
Austria	Japan	Republic
Denmark	Norway	United Kingdom
Hungary	Sweden	
Canada	Luxembourg	

| 7 |

Privatization of Social Security

As was mentioned in the introduction to this text, the worker to beneficiary ratio is falling due to the retirement of the baby boomers. Meanwhile, one of Social Security's principle trust funds, the Disability Insurance (DI) Trust Fund will run out of cash reserves next year. The trust fund has 10.9 billion beneficiaries as of November 2014. Without cash reserves, the benefits for these beneficiaries will need to be cut by about 20% in 2016 to ensure the program's solvency. Meanwhile the other major Social Security trust fund, the OASDI (Old Age Survivors and Disability Insurance) Trust is positioned to burn through all of its cash reserves by 2033. If nothing is done to repair the cash flows of these trust funds, then the overall cut to Social Security benefits would have to be around 25 percent in order for the program to stay solvent.

For well over a decade, how best to manage the Social Security program in the future has been the center of many spirited debates. Politicians with more liberal leanings argue that the program should be preserved as is, and that the program's financial solvency should be given the highest priority, even if it means raising taxes or diverting other federal funds. The conservative political element has continuously invited Americans to consider the possibility of allowing seniors to invest a portion of their Social Security withholdings in the stock market. This latter option has come to be known as the ***privatization*** of Social Security and is a political hot button.

Those in favor of privatization point out that the rate of return received by retirees has much more growth potential in the stock market, and if more seniors have larger retirement accounts, then they're apt to spend more, which will lead to more tax revenue and is good overall for the economy. Furthermore, if even a small portion of the money currently going into Social Security (about 840 billion dollars annually) were redirected into the stock market that too could be good for the overall economy.

Proponents of privatization also cite the relative political expediency of tackling Social Security's financial problems by way of privatization. The only other apparent alternatives to maintain the long-term solvency of the program are either to cut benefits or raise Social Security taxes, both of which would be met with significant political opposition.

One of the biggest obstacles to privatization is the fact that Social Security has decades worth of liabilities to workers who've paid into the system, totaling in the trillions of dollars. Currently, the system works in a pay-as-you-go fashion; money is collected from the payroll of active workers, and that same money is immediately distributed to retirees. If we were to suddenly begin putting Social Security withholdings in the stock market, how would we pay the program's 59 million beneficiaries? That money would no longer exist as cash on hand, but would be tied up in investment accounts (a term known as illiquidity, or the inability to access one's own money).

Privatization would force the government to find a way to simultaneously allow current workers to pay into the stock market and provide Social Security beneficiaries with the benefits they were promised. Most plans that have been proposed to privatize Social Security come with massive federal borrowing measures to bridge the gap between the investment of cash and the disbursement of cash to beneficiaries. Other proposed plans are slightly more inventive and agile by way of calling for the current cash reserves in Social Security to be invested in private equity accounts.

How Privatized Social Security Works

In a privatized Social Security system, every individual payee would have his or her own private benefits account. Currently, the government maintains a series of trust funds from which Social Security benefits are paid. With a privatized system, workers would be the sole owners of their accounts. They would also be allowed to make decisions about how they want their money invested. Just like the current system, workers would be allowed to withdraw money from their accounts only after they reached retirement age or if they became disabled. In the event that a worker died before withdrawing all of his or her funds from the privatized Social Security account in that person's name, he or she could bequeath the remainder of the account's assets to heirs of his or her choosing.

This system would be quite different from the current system with its very specific rules governing survivor benefits. In fact, this change would have very interesting implications. If everyone currently contributing to social security began contributing to a private, stock market-based fund instead, then some individuals—from all socio-economic demographics—would do quite well and others—also from all socio-economic demographics—not so well. Given that beneficiaries could leave their remaining assets to whomever they choose, there would likely be a much more broad dispersion of inherited retirement assets than there is currently in the status quo.

As we discussed in detail in Chapter 1, minorities and persons of color are more likely to be more dependent on Social Security than white males. If a segment of privatized Social Security accounts matured significantly, and there would be no way to predict which ones would, the current socio economic environment would be thrown upside down. These account *maturations* and growths would happen largely at random and many of these assets would be passed down to successive generations. It is then conceivable that the overall wealth distribution disparity between whites and minorities and persons of color would inevitably shrink, and the scales would tip toward an even center.

Under some mock-ups for Social Security privatization, workers would be required to deposit their Social Security withholdings into one of a handful of approved funds. Having a limited range of funds would lower the inherent risk of stock market investment, and consequently the potential for high figure growth. Examples of funds that might be recommended for Social Security investors include: money market funds, stock index funds, real estate investment trusts, corporate bond funds, and US Treasury bond funds—all of which are known to be stable though they often bring low returns.

Yet another strategy would, ironically enough, look and feel similar to today's Affordable Care Act (commonly referred to as Obamacare). Existing investment companies would compete to develop Social Security funds that would attract worker contributions. This strategy would grant a high degree of flexibility to the workforce, but the administrative costs would be high as a reflection of the fact that so many workers would enter into retirement with highly disparate retirement accounts. One thing about the status quo Social Security system that allows it to operate so efficiently—incurring only 1 percent in administrative costs relative to the total amount of benefits paid out—is the fact that everyone pays into the same system, and the money, for all intents and purposes, is paid into and taken out of the same financial pool.

One of the factors that keeps the privatization debate alive in the United States is the fact that other countries, when faced with similar difficulties keeping their Social Security equivalents financially solvent, have also resorted to privatization with considerable success. Chile, for instance, has transitioned into a partially private system that's much more cost-effective and capable of providing its population with a more stable stream of benefits. Likewise, the UK has seen success moving its Social Security equivalent revenues into private pension funds.

When it comes to receipt of benefits post-retirement, a privatized system would have two fundamental distinctions from the current system. Firstly, the worker's retirement benefit would depend on the size of his or her contributions and the growth of the investments made. Secondly, the actual funds received from retirement investments will be the same money that was originally invested. This is known as **advance funding** and contrasts with Social Security's current pay-as-you-go model in which the funds paid are the same as those being contributed currently by today's workforce. Assuming steady growth in the stock market, a private system would result in higher payouts from retirement accounts across the board.

One of the unique and beneficial aspects of Social Security's current system is the progressive distribution of benefits that favors low wage earners and single income couples. Even though lower-income retirees don't get paid as much, their overall payouts from the system relative to what they contributed over the course of their working lives is a highly favorable ratio. A privatized advance pay system would not duplicate this progressive distribution because retirees would simply receive the matured accumulation of the funds invested into the program over the *Continued on following page...* course of their working lives. Under this system higher earners would find themselves with dramatically larger retirement accounts than lower earners assuming there are not interventions put in place. This would be the result of the simple fact that lower earners would not have as much to invest. In order to mimic the progressive distribution quality of the old (current) system, the privatized system would have to be amended with tax-based supplements to boost the retirement payouts of the lower-wage earners.

While privatization of Social Security may indeed promise significant improvement to the overall quality of retirement in America, its most significant obstacle is filling the gap between current retirees who've already paid into the system and are expecting to receive their benefits, and a current workforce that can't simultaneously finance the Social Security system while also financing a separate new private retirement program. Doing so would essentially equate to forcing the current workforce to finance both their own retirements as well as those of the current generation of retirees, a move that would bankrupt the retirement funds of all but the highest earners of the current workforce. Most economists agree that the transition could not be accomplished without a 'consumption sacrifice', meaning that either the working population will be taxed more, that the retired population will receive fewer retirement benefits, or a combination of both. In conclusion, the benefits of a transition to a more privatized system would probably be significant, but there are no easy roads in sight to take us there.

Chapter Recap

fig.10

The Debate to Privatize Social Security			
The Issue	Currently there is an unsustainable ratio of retirees to members of the current workforce. This means that over time the funds that provide money for Social Security benefits will dry up and there will be insufficient funding for new retirees.		
What is Privatization?	Instead of a pay-as-you-go system, workers would pay into personal accounts that are invested into the stock market	The growth of the funds in these personal accounts would provide the money needed for comfortable retirement	
Why Privatization?	Privatization has the potential to alleviate the current predicament facing Social Security's fast disappearing funds	The random nature of market and account growth could change the socioeconomic status for many Americans and help close the widening wealth gap	
Why not Privatization?	All investments carry some risk	There is currently no progressive method to protect low earners	There is no clear path to implementation of a privatized system without the current workforce unfairly bearing the brunt of the costs

| 8 |

Other Potential Changes

If you're approaching retirement age, or even if you're just trying to be a diligent and smart financial planner, then you should know about what changes may impact the Social Security system in the near future. Here are a few recent topics that have garnered quite a bit of discussion:

Improving Benefits

Some argue that Social Security does not adequately cover certain vulnerable groups and that benefits should be improved accordingly. For example, consider a 25-year-old young adult who's spent the last three years living at home taking care of an aging or unwell parent. In the event he or she becomes disabled, the 25-year-old would not have acquired the requisite credits needed to qualify for disability benefits. Some believe the answer to this problem is to provide a way by which individuals who are not part of the paid workforce can still earn credits for caring for a child or another family member.

Other ideas for improving benefits include establishing a 'new minimum benefit' specifically designed to help people who've worked their entire lives in low-paying careers. Even though, proportionately, the Social Security system awards lower earners with a larger percentage allotment relative to their working salaries, if a person earned only $20,000 a year for his whole career and is less likely to have other outside retirement investments, then he's suddenly asked to live off of about $11,000 a year, or to keep working indefinitely past age 66. The new minimum benefit policy would raise the benefit amount for those life-long low earners who deserve a reasonable retirement just as much as anyone else.

Other proponents of reform claim that the current survivor's benefit is not adequate, as it currently only awards the surviving spouse a proportion of the deceased spouse's benefits. Another existing proposal seeks to expand the benefits for children whose parents become disabled, which could be implemented by allowing these children to continue to receive benefits until age 22 if they are in college or vocational school.

Conservative-minded politicians and think tanks with similar values argue that the benefits of Social Security should only be expanded in conjunction with a comprehensive reform that ensures the program's financial solvency. Adjusting benefits upward now, they argue, would deplete the Social Security trust funds more rapidly. This rapid depletion would lead to a situation in which benefits across the board have to be cut. This would essentially mean that making allowances to help some specific vulnerable parties could in effect reduce benefits for all Americans receiving Social Security benefits. Instead of tinkering with the benefits piecemeal, they argue, all benefits packages and funding mechanisms should be reviewed and reformed to ensure that the program will thrive financially and survive indefinitely. Once the system is in a more stable financial position it will then be easier to address the issue of parties that may be unfairly left out of the system.

Raising the Full Retirement Age (FRA)

In 1983, in the wake of the Greenspan Commission, Congress determined that the full retirement age for Social Security beneficiaries would need to steadily increase over time to help the program stay fully flush financially and to account for the reality that the average lifespan of the population would similarly increase. In 1985, 65 was the full retirement age. Now, for retirees born in the year 1960 or later, the FRA age is 67. As time goes on the retirement age is scheduled to rise even further. Some believe that this trend of raising the retirement age should continue long after the initial provisions laid out by the Greenspan commission expire.

One specific proposal calls for 68 to be the new full retirement age and proposes that, beginning in 2023, the retirement age should be increased by two months each year. By the year 2028, 68 would be the new 67. It may not seem like such a dramatic shift, but the estimates say that this small tweak could repair up to 18 percent of the funding gap.

Another FRA-raising proposal goes even further, suggesting that 70 is the best target age. This proposal, like the former, would begin its ascension in 2023, and increase the retirement age by two months each year until 2040. Such a change would result in an estimated 44 percent repair of the funding gap. Proponents of raising the FRA point not only to the financial benefits, but also to the inevitability of our lifespans increasing over time in the modern age. Failing to raise the FRA commits the program to supporting longer and longer retirements, and that doesn't make good financial sense, especially considering the scarcity of funds.

Opponents of raising the FRA, such as Virginia Reno of the National Academy of Social Insurance, frame the change as a type of benefits cut. Reno points out that current law increasing the FRA from 65 to 67 is essentially a 13 percent benefit cut. Perhaps most poignant is the argument that low-earning workers have seen little to no gains in their longevity since 1935, which in turn makes extending the FRA seem unfair to the those of us who occupy the lowest socioeconomic strata in society.

Increasing the Payroll Tax Rate

When a tax-based program needs money, just raise the tax, right? Not exactly. Many Americans feel that taxes are too high as it is. Not to mention that higher taxes lead to less consumer spending—one of the major driving forces of the US economy. As we covered in previous chapters, employees and employers currently each pay 6.2% of payroll earnings into Social Security for up to $110,000 of earned income.

Self-employed persons pay a total of 12.4%of their earnings up to the $110,000 cap.

One proposal to aid Social Security's financial woes with a payroll tax increase is a plan that would increase both the employer and employee share to 6.45% (12.90% combined). While this may seem like a small change, if it were enacted immediately, it would repair 22 percent of the program's current funding gap without any change to the FRA. Another proposal goes even further, arguing that 7.2% is the right number (a full 1%increase). Since this would be a larger tax hike, it would need to be executed over the course of 20 years, but projections show that such a move would repair the funding gap by a whopping 64 percent. If this tax increase is coupled with even the least aggressive increases to the FRA, we could see significant improvements to the current Social Security predicament.

For the average earner, raising the tax rate to 7.2% would only cost 50 cents more per week while making a landmark improvement to the financial wellbeing of Social Security and closing over half of the program's funding gap. For larger earners and corporations, however, paying a full half a percent more on payroll tax represents a significant investment and won't be quite as popular an idea.

Because corporations wield so much political power, an increase to payroll tax becomes a very tricky political hurdle. And this isn't simply a matter of greed. If payroll taxes get too expensive than the price of having employees becomes too expensive and corporations are inclined to replace more and more human laborers with machines where possible. Another constant political threat hanging over federal policy makers is that more and more businesses that operate in the US will move their manufacturing departments to countries where labor is not as expensive. The reality of a free country is that businesses, large corporations or otherwise, are free to operate and relocate at will— and if they're Schedule C corporations, then they're legally bound to maximize profit. If employers lay off workers due to unmanageable or even merely unprofitable payroll tax developments, then the pay-as-you-go Social Security system will lose many working-age contributors to unemployment via replacement or outsourcing. The result would be an even more fettered Social Security program, the opposite of the intended effect. Understanding the realities of corporate incentives in relation to payroll tax is critical to the promotion of good policy.

Reducing Benefits for Higher Earners

If a person has consistently made a high salary while putting forth the effort required to retire with a quality of life similar to what he or she enjoyed as during that person's time as a member of the workforce person, then the benefits that individual receives from Social Security probably won't make a huge difference to his or her overall retirement plan. The question is whether or not this is fair to the person who, regardless of salary size, has been contributing significant sums to this fund for his or her entire working life. In the status quo, the proportion of benefits received relative to the amount paid in is already much lower in the case of higher-income earners. In many countries, wealthier citizens pay much more in taxes to fund programs that benefit the poor and only the poor.

One proposed option reduces the benefits of the highest earning 25 percent of Social Security beneficiaries by about 15%. This modest reduction in benefits for the country's top earners will repair 7 percent of the funding gap. Another option is to cut benefits for the upper 50 percent of the population according to a sliding scale, with those at the very top seeing a 28 percent reduction of their benefits. This more comprehensive benefits approach, though more likely to impact the middle class, is estimated to fill about 31 percent of the current Social Security funding gap. Yet another proposed plan is to make Social Security benefits contingent upon the amount of retirement income being derived from other sources. If a person who earned an average $50,000 during the course of his lifetime finds himself taking in $75,000 annually from a well-matured 401(k), then he could probably withstand a 15 percent reduction in his Social Security benefits.

Longevity Indexing

Another potential fix for Social Security's financial woes is to initiate a policy of *longevity indexing*. Longevity indexing is distinct from simply raising the full retirement age, because rather than simply changing the age at which retirees can begin receiving full benefits, indexing would use longevity data to reduce the amount of benefits awarded in proportion to life expectancy. The more years a beneficiary is expected to live, the fewer benefits per year he or she would receive, though the total benefits package would still be in line with that individual's expected full entitlement amount.

Simply put, rather than look the other way while people continue to live and collect Social Security for longer and longer periods, indexing longevity would balance out benefits paid to accommodate longer lifespans. Such a change is estimated to repair 20-26 percent of Social Security's current funding gap.

Detractors of this method use a similar argument to the one they use to detract the idea of a straight raise for the FRA: just because some people are living longer doesn't mean everyone should be subject to a decrease in benefits. The cost of healthcare continues to increase, as does rent and food, while the value of standard retirement assets, such as homes, pensions, and life savings are not available or are at-risk for many retirees—especially those retirees who were lifetime low earners. Couple that with the fact that low-income earners have not been privy to the same increase in longevity as their more affluent counterparts, and the idea of watering down benefits on the basis of indexed longevity seems very unfair to lower-income retirees.

Adjusting the COLA Calculation Method

The Consumer Price Index is the main reference point used when calculating Social Security's Cost of Living Adjustment (COLA), which ensures that Social Security payouts keep pace with modern living expenses. An interesting argument can be made that a 'chained' Consumer Price Index would better serve the system. A chained Consumer Price Index would not only account for the changing costs of goods and services, but would also account for the adjustments consumers make to their spending habits in response to these changes. Some estimates show that the Social Security COLA adjustment, if calculated using a chained Consumer Price Index, would increase benefits by a smaller amount. Over time, this more modest uptick in the benefits payout could possibly lead to significant savings.

Another COLA calculation method is the 'Elderly Index', which accounts specifically for the spending habits of older Americans in response to the rise and fall of living costs. Since many older Americans spend a disproportionate amount of money on healthcare services, use of the Elderly Index tends to adjust COLA projections upward rather than downward. If we were to use this index, then we'd likely end up paying more in benefits over time and further widening the program's funding gap. Though it's an inconvenient truth, the Elderly Index is the most accurate and targeted way of inferring the economic realities of senior citizens. There's no denying the fact that older Americans pay more out-of-pocket healthcare expenses and that the cost of healthcare rises faster than the rate of inflation.

Other Salary Reductions

Thanks to a reform congress passed in 1983, certain salary reduction plans, such as the employer-sponsored 401(k), are subject to Social Security withholding. Other salary reduction plans, such as Flexible Spending Accounts, are not taxable. If the government taxed the currently non-taxable plans and subjected them to both the employee and employer share of the standard Social Security withholding (6.2% each), then it is estimated that the additional tax revenue would fill approximately 10 percent of Social Security's funding gap. Furthermore, the parties who pay Social Security taxes on their currently non-taxable plans will be adding more to their base earning levels, meaning that their own Social Security payouts will be greater when they retire.

The drawback to this proposed change is that the non-taxable status of these plans is their greatest incentive for employers. If we were to start taxing them, then fewer employers would offer them, fewer employees would benefit from them, and the projected tax revenue would shrink.

Coverage for Government Workers

Currently, 25% of state and local government workers do not pay into Social Security. They receive separate retirement programs run by the state or local authority. If newly-hired state and local government workers were required to pay into Social Security, just like all US workers in the private sector, then we'd have a chance for a relatively seamless transition into a greater overall network of program contributors. Perhaps now—with the retirement of the baby boomers—is the best time to instigate this transition. If executed, this change would repair about 8 percent of the current Social Security funding gap.

One potential repercussion from the execution of this change would be the stress it would put on the local and state-level retirement programs, which are also dependent on the contributions of younger workers to ensure their solvency. If Social Security were to snatch away the next generation of contributors, then the benefits of current state and local retirees would be in jeopardy. The state and local authorities would likely resort to tax hikes in order to repair the loss of funding for their retirement programs. As we discussed earlier in this chapter, the unforeseen or long-term effects of tax increases can do more harm than good if implemented poorly.

Expanding the Number of Working Years

Currently, a Social Security beneficiary's benefits are based on his or her average income over the 35 years in which that worker earned the highest amount. If the worker does not earn income for 35 years, then each year less than 35 factors in as a zero in the calculation of the average. Riding the trend of increasing longevity and a higher FRA, it seems an increase in the number of working years assessed to 38 or 40 may also be in order. A longer span of assessment would result in an overall decrease in the average earnings, and thus a decrease in the average Social Security payout. It's estimated that expanding the average computation to account for 38 years would repair 13 percent of Social Security's funding gap. This change would also encourage young people to begin working and planning for their retirements earlier. As always, the system becomes more flexible and more solvent when more contributions are coming from younger workers.

Critics of this calculation change again point to the plight of the lower income earners, the less educated, and many women, who would be most adversely impacted by the change. The benefits reduction, they argue, would not only reduce the retirement benefits of the principle earners, but also of their spouses and dependents.

Means Testing

Means testing, one of the most direct yet controversial approaches to making a dent in the Social Security funding gap, applies a Marxist style threshold to beneficiaries to determine how much, if any, of their benefits would be payable. Means testing is more than a reduction of benefits for higher-income earners, in that a person's eligibility to receive benefits would be contingent upon his or her current income situation. For example, if he or she receives money from current employment, or from other retirement income sources, then that person's Social Security income would be adjusted or eliminated accordingly. Implementing a reasonable means-testing policy would instantly repair the funding gap by 10 percent.

This approach is so controversial because it essentially translates into a straight 6% (12% for the self-employed) tax hike for higher-income Americans. These individuals would pay into the system but receive little or nothing for their contributions. In the United States, this degree of wealth redistribution is considered extreme. Proponents of means testing argue that in this era of debt and limited financial resource, we simply can't afford to pay unneeded retirement benefits that equate to coffee money for our nation's wealthiest individuals, when that same money could be used as the financial lifeblood for many struggling retirees.

In addition to bringing up philosophical challenges, detractors also point out that means testing would increase Social Security's administrative overhead. In order to verify wealth and income, government employees would have to continuously monitor and check in on the employment and wealth status of all retired Americans, which is not a small task. Furthermore, for middle income Americans, the incentive to independently plan for retirement would be reduced if they knew that thousands of dollars in retracted Social Security benefits would have to be accounted for before any real improvements were made to the overall retirement picture.

Striking a Good Balance

Entitlement reform of any kind is always going to be a highly politicized endeavor. People have worked for decades expecting to receive the benefits they were promised. Nonetheless, changes must be made if the Social Security program is to remain financially solvent.

Another tweaking point that could really make a big impact with relatively little cost is abolishing the earnings cap on Social Security taxes in lieu of raising the payroll tax. As was discussed in Chapter 7, the problem with raising payroll taxes across the board is that employers may respond by mechanizing the younger and lower-skilled workforce or by moving operations overseas, leading to layoffs, unemployment and an even further reduction of the workforce currently paying into the Social Security program. But if the earnings cap were removed instead, then the payroll tax would only be raised for those making upwards of $110,000 annually, not for lower-income earners. Proceeding with the safe assumption that individuals at this salary are performing jobs that aren't as easily mechanized, there would be less risk of layoffs than there would be if we raised taxes on across-the-board payroll.

This particular combination of changes would be politically expedient, seeing as abolishing the earnings cap would, on balance, benefit lower-income Americans. As for accepting the fact that people are living longer and adjusting Social Security accordingly, this would be less popular with lower-income Americans who are less likely to be able to retire before they're eligible for Social Security benefits. Furthermore, as was mentioned several times in this book, some statistics indicate that the observed expansion in longevity has strongly favored middle and upper class Americans. Nonetheless, in conjunction with abolishing the earnings cap, and perhaps while also encouraging healthier work environments and personal behaviors, the extension of full retirement age is appropriate and reasonable.

Across the Board Support

While there is a panoply of opinions and recommendations for the future of Social Security, it is fairly clear that not only does the program benefit Americans, but those on both sides of the aisle believe that there should be a future for Social Security.

Based on this evidence, the most strongly conservative Americans don't want to see cuts, the most liberal don't want to see cuts, and moderates on both sides are more inclined to support the continuation of Social Security rather than see it cut. This shows that the future of Social Security is not up for political debate; it is rather up for more level-headed and productive discourse. The question is, should Social Security be expanded to cover more Americans or should it be left as is? For those millions of Americans who rely in Social Security as their primary or only source of income, this is very good news.

It is also worth noting that at a time when political divisiveness seems to be at an all-time high all around us, many Americans still agree on the fact that an investment in their own futures is a very beneficial thing.

Few People Support Phasing out Social Security		
Affiliation	*Benefits Should Not be Reduced in Any Way*	*Reductions Should be Considered for the Future*
All	67% with 27% saying it should be expanded to cover more Americans	31% with 6% saying it should be cut as a gov't program
Consistently Conservative	59% with 12% saying it should be expanded	38% with 12% saying it should be cut
Mostly Conservative	59% with 16% saying it should be expanded	37% with 8% saying it should be cut
Mixed	70% with 29% saying it should be expanded	28% with 6% saying it should be cut
Mostly Liberal	69% with 35% saying it should be expanded	29% with 6% saying it should be cut
Consistently Liberal	66% with 31% saying it should be expanded	32% with 2% saying it should be cut

fig. 11 : Source: 2014 Pew Poll of the American Public. Note that responses classified as 'i don't know' are not shown. Political affiliation and values based on a scale of 10 questions.

191
Roth IRAs

When undertaking your financial planning, whether on your own or with the assistance of a financial planner or consultant, it is important to understand the distinction between traditional IRAs and Roth IRAs. The primary difference between the two is when your money is taxed.

A Roth IRA is a retirement savings account that allows your money to grow tax-free. It is funded with after-tax dollars, and when you withdraw your money there is no tax applied to it, no matter how much it may have grown.

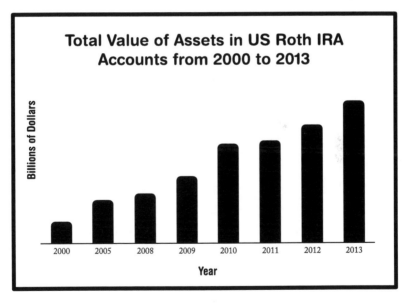

 fig. 12 : The trend of increasing contributions to Roth IRA accounts. Source: Statista

This is the direct opposite of a traditional IRA, which funds your retirement savings account with pre-tax money then taxes the withdrawals when you are in your retirement years, though both accounts allow your money to grow without being subject to annual taxes.

Roth IRAs also offer more flexibility than traditional IRAs. While the latter has a 'required minimum distributions' clause that forces you to start making withdrawals when you reach age 70½, the Roth version lets you leave your money for as long as you see fit. Additionally, traditional IRAs prohibit contributions after age 70½ while Roth IRAs allow continual contributions regardless of age.

All of these advantages make the Roth IRA seem like a clear winner when it comes to retirement planning, but there are some things to keep in mind. Roth IRAs are subject to income limits. Individuals or couples who make more than the limit are ineligible for the Roth version and therefore can only participate in traditional IRAs. As of 2015, individuals are only eligible to participate in a Roth IRA if their incomes are less than $105,000. That number jumps to $167,000 for married couples filing jointly.

With questions of eligibility out of the way, there are some other considerations to examine. If you expect to be in a lower tax bracket when you retire, a traditional IRA lowers your current tax bill (remember, traditional IRAs are funded with pre-tax earnings) and later when it is withdrawn it will be subject to the taxes of a lower tax bracket.

The inverse is true if you expect to be in a higher tax bracket when retirement comes around. Choosing a Roth IRA means that settling your taxes now ultimately benefits you. The taxes are assessed against your current earnings bracket, then your money grows and you are able to withdraw when you're older and skip the higher-bracket taxes.

Of course it can be nearly impossible to make that determination if you are in your thirties, or even your forties. The best advice financial consultants give is to keep a tax diversified retirement savings portfolio. That means contributing to funds that are both taxed and tax-free upon withdrawal (if you qualify). While it may not maximize your tax benefit or most effectively capitalize on the characteristics of either retirement savings option, it is the safest option that prepares for either eventuality.

conclusion

Social Security, in many ways, has all the qualities of an ideal pension plan. It's a portable retirement plan that will follow you from job to job. It is designed to keep up with inflation, and will keep paying you for as long as you live. Be that as it may, Social Security is a highly modest fund, which only pays $1,230 a month on average. For the large group of Americans depending on Social Security as their primary source of retirement income, the program's bare bones benefits package leaves them with a significant amount of financial hardship to bare.

One thing that cannot be ignored, though it's often easy to do so, is the age of the Social Security program. It's been around since 1935, a time when the average 65-year-old man was expected to live another 13 years before dying. Women at this time averaged about 15 years after 65. Raising the retirement age is just as sensible and crucial to the program's solvency as raising the amount of benefits paid in order to account for inflation.

No matter what the eventual outcome of the Social Security debate, the fact remains that what is at stake is not to be trifled with: the sunset years of some of America's hardest workers. It behooves us as citizens to understand the ways in which Social Security currently helps us, the ways it could better help us, and the course that the program could potentially take.

Citizens across America agree: Social Security is important. The degree to which it should receive funding and the age at which beneficiaries may begin receiving their penalty-free payments are the minutia under debate. Whatever the decisions we are called upon to make are, the best decision we can make is an informed one. That is especially true considering the gravity and weight of retirement planning.

I hope that this book was informative for you and now you're ready to really benefit the in expansion of your knowledge concerning the Social Security system.

For more information & government-provided resources concerning Social Security, visit the website at:

www.ssa.gov

glossary

Advance Funding-
A privatized alternative to the current pay-as-you-go Social Security funding method. Advance funding takes contributions from workforce paychecks and invests them in the market. The growth is then used to fund the retirement of the worker. Advance funding means that the actual payout for each worker could vary radically based on the performance of his or her money and the accumulated growth when they decide to retire.

After Tax Income-
Your 'after tax income', also called 'actual income' is the value of your paycheck less any taxes. It is your take home pay after taxes.

Compound Interest-
Interest that is calculated based on the value of the principal plus any interest already accrued. For example, in the first period of an account with compound interest, interest is only calculated on the principal amount. In the second period it is calculated on the principal plus the interest already accrued, treating this total value as the new principal.

Cost of Living Adjustment (COLA)-
A method by which a retiree may state a claim for her Social Security benefits but delay payments of the benefits for another few years.

Disability Insurance (DI)-
The name of one of Social Security's main trust funds. The DI is a separate account in the US treasury and is used to finance disabled worker benefits.

Federal Insurance Contributions Act (FICA)-
The payroll tax used to collect Social Security contributions from employees and employers.

File & Suspend-
A method by which a retiree may state a claim for Social Security benefits but delay payments of the benefits for another few years. This approach ensures payable benefits begin to accumulate and are available in the event of an injury or other emergency.

Full Retirement Age (FRA)-
The age at which a Social Security beneficiary is eligible to begin receiving her full benefit amount. She can also elect to begin receiving benefit distributions before reaching her FRA, though she'll receive less than her full benefit amount for the duration of her life. She can elect to begin receiving benefits after surpassing her FRA, and she will receive a larger benefit amount.

Gross Domestic Product (GDP)-
The total value of the goods and services produced within a country over a set period such as annually or quarterly. The GDP value is a primary indicator of the strength and size of a nation's economy.

Inflation-
Inflation is the natural devaluing of a nation's currency over time. As currency buys less and less, the cost of goods and services rises. The standard rate of inflation fluctuates between 1 and 3% annually.

Longevity Indexing-
The practice of adjusting benefits payout to account for statistical life expectancy.

Maturation (of a loan)-
When a loan is 'due' it is considered mature. The maturity of a loan is the point at which the full value of the loan and all interest is due.

Old Age and Survivor's Insurance (OASI)-
The name of one of Social Security's main trust funds. The OASI is a separate account in the US treasury and is used to finance Social Security retirees' benefits.

Pay-As-You-Go-
A financing methodology employed by Social Security whereby the Social Security contributions of today's workers are used to pay for the benefits of today's retirees. Pay-as-you-go is separate from "advance funding" of retirement, whereby money paid into an account, or invested into a stock, fund, 401(k) or IRA is left alone to mature over the years.

Primary Insurance Amount (PIA)-
The total benefit amount one is eligible to receive upon reaching one's full retirement age (FRA).

Principle (of a loan)-
The initial amount that a loan starts with. This is the initial amount that interest is calculated on.

Privatization-
The act of changing the Social Security program from a pay-as-you-go system to a system which benefits from advanced funding or the process of investing retirement savings in the market and using the growth to fund Social Security. There are criticisms of privatization including concerns that no sector of the market is stable enough to entrust with the futures of retiring Americans, and that the added administrative costs would be wasteful expenditure.

Progressive Benefit Formula-
A system that determines Social Security payouts whereby lower income payees receive a higher proportion of their working life income paid out in the form of Social Security benefits.

Replacement Rates-
The name of one of Social Security's main The percentage value of a person's Social Security income in relation to the average income that person received during his working life—the amount of income that is replaced by Social Security benefits. Individuals who've had lower lifetime earnings tend to have larger replacement rates, as a greater percentage of their lost working income is replaced by Social Security during their retirement.

Self-Employed Contributions Act (SECA)-
The proportion of a self-employed person's net earnings that's paid into Social Security. Self-employed persons are responsible for paying more Social Security tax than employees, whose contributions are matched by their employers. Self-employed persons may deduct the employer's share (1/2) of their SECA tax as a business expense.

Social Security Administration (SSA)-
The federal government bureau responsible for Social Security. A relatively efficient bureaucracy, the entire operational expense of SSA is less than 1percent of the total amount of Social Security benefits paid.

Windfall Elimination Provision (WEP)-
A method of preventing workers who became eligible for Social Security benefits but who did not pay FICA taxes from collecting benefits from a pool that they never paid into. Primarily affects government and non-profit employees.

about clydebank

We are a multi-media publishing company that provides reliable, high-quality and easily accessible information to a global customer base. Developed out of the need for beginner-friendly content that is accessible across multiple formats, we deliver reliable, up-to-date, high-quality information through our multiple product offerings.

Through our strategic partnerships with some of the world's largest retailers, we are able to simplify the learning process for customers around the world, providing them with an authoritative source of information for the subjects that matter to them. Our end-user focused philosophy puts the satisfaction of our customers at the forefront of our mission. We are committed to creating multi-media products that allow our customers to learn what they want, when they want and how they want.

ClydeBank Finance is a division of the multimedia-publishing firm ClydeBank Media LLC. ClydeBank Media's goal is to provide affordable, accessible information to a global market through different forms of media such as eBooks, paperback books and audio books. Company divisions are based on subject matter, each consisting of a dedicated team of researchers, writers, editors and designers.

For more information, please visit us at :
www.clydebankmedia.com
or contact *info@clydebankmedia.com*

Your world, simplified.

notes

STAY INFORMED

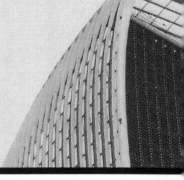

ClydeBank FINANCE | BLOG

Your Source for All Things Finance

Why Should I Sign Up for the Mailing List?

- Get a $10 ClydeBank Media gift card!
- Be the first to know about new products
- Receive exclusive promotions & discounts

Stay on top of the latest finance trends by joining our free mailing list today at:

www.clydebankmedia.com/finance-blog

53083954R00060

Made in the USA
San Bernardino, CA
05 September 2017